TRYING . . . FOR 55 YEARS

SOME LEGAL CASES THAT EFFECTED THE LAW
AND AFFECTED THE LAWYER

MICHAEL D. SCHOTTLAND, ESQ.

WC Publishing
an On-Target Words Imprint

DEDICATION

To my wife, Rosanne, for a life's work of patience and understanding.

A REVIEW OF THE BOOK
By Leonard Birdsong, JD

Mr. Schottland is obviously a man of courage, as well as a skilled man of the law. I don't know him personally, but I say this because of the book he has written.

Many people in our society do not like lawyers, probably because they don't know of the good work that the honest, ethical and hardworking lawyers like Mr. Schottland have provided serving their clients and the law through their careers. We need more lawyers who write like Mr. Schottland who provides us with the wisdom that a democracy like ours requires. He is a man of courage because he has had the insight to write a biography like only a few before him. The facts and experiences shared in the cases he presents herein are those remembered by the author and captured by the author in notes made over these many years. Such is the case with all autobiographical writings, but this work exposes the variety and types of cases and their problems which other lawyers young and old may use as an inspirational road map or template for their own practices' and careers.

His journey begins the year after he graduates from Rutgers Law School when he was asked to represent two of four senior Rutgers law students accused of cribbing on a final exam in tax law that Spring. A friend was one of those accused. However, that friend's family employed a senior partner of a well-respected Newark firm to represent him and one other of the accused. They admitted their cheating, and both lost a year, having to return and graduate the following year.

Mr. Schottland's clients insisted they were innocent, so four professors were empaneled to hear the case. The assistant dean acted as prosecutor and main witness. Schottland had to cross-examine this man who only a year earlier, when he was a student, held a dominant position of power over him. This change in roles, though a little scary, freed and empowered Schottland to use the skills against some of the very panel members who had taught him. His cross-examination revealed the assistant dean's allegations were based on mere hearsay and assumptions which could not stand as legal evidence. As a result, his clients were exonerated and allowed to graduate. He reveals that this case was quite an eye opener for him: "Sheer transformation. From theory to practice." He then knew what he could do and announces, "ladies and gentlemen start your engines!"

In one of his next cases he recalls a personal injury case in which we learn he won his first million-dollar verdict. He then goes on to write about many other interesting clients and trials such as clients charged with murder, cases involving conscientious objectors during the Viet Nam era, labor law cases, and horse race commission cases. The last case he writes about is a sad personal injury matter which involved a child suffering the lifetime effects of oxygen deprivation suffered during a flawed labor and delivery that could and should have been avoided. What a varied practice! I recommend this book to lawyers and all others who wish to learn more about how our legal system really works.

Mr. Schottland has been a member of the Monmouth Bar Association for many years and served as Chairman of its Civil Practice Committee and is a member emeritus of the New Jersey State Bar Association. Over his career, which has spanned more than fifty years, he has achieved several substantial and notable results in the courts. He is currently active in malpractice matters, general civil litigation and cases related to racing law. He is the father of five children, grandfather of ten, and resides in New Jersey with his wife, Rosanne.

Leonard Birdsong is a lawyer and retired Law Professor. He is the author of *Professor Birdsong's Law School Guide: Techniques for Choosing and Applying to Law School"*. He may be contacted at lbirdsong22@gmail.com

Table of Contents

PREFACE

I was one of those kids who, from an early age, knew he wanted to become a lawyer. My grandfather was a lawyer and my father, was a frustrated non-lawyer. Over the course of my fifty plus years of practice, I've been blessed, working with some wonderful associates, experts, and the individuals and families of those I represented.

Attorneys who specialize in litigation get a bum rap, and when the media hypes some rare instance of a recovery seemingly out of step with real injury, lawyers are broadly brushed as the root of all that is wrong in the American justice system. Few of the media, and even fewer of the critics have ever looked into the eyes of a crippled mother, felt a parent's undying love of a child who will never speak, walk or otherwise take care of himself, or have seen how a sudden, violent and unnecessary death changes a family forever.

Lawyers know neither money nor justice will cure pain, but we seek both because that is all we can do to help. When a jury returns a verdict finding someone at fault for causing someone else's loss, we are not attacking core American values, we are upholding them! There must be personal responsibility.

This book began as a diary of my own journey as an attorney, with no thought of doing anything other than capturing my experiences, lest they fade with memory. It was the encouragement of colleagues, family and friends that turned me towards sharing my experiences with interested people.

The material is organized by cases, but I have tried not to get bogged down with procedural matters unless they were key to the message. As I read through this from start to finish, I noticed changes in my own philosophies, style of representation and case selection. What I hope comes through, in all instances, is how much I love being a lawyer, and how thrilling it is to do battle in a just cause and succeed for that cause. If you don't have a passion for justice, then you cannot succeed in this legal environment.

What was my legal career spanning fifty years all about? This writing is an attempt to respond to that question.

I attended law school at Rutgers-Newark, a member of an experimental program comparing how students without four-year undergraduate degrees did against those with a full baccalaureate. At the time, New Jersey permitted entry to the bar with only three-quarters of the credits necessary for that undergraduate degree. I passed the bar exam in 1965; the passage rate back then was 39%.

I thought my career path would be an Appellate Division clerkship, then a job in the office of the Attorney General of New Jersey. Instead, I started as a lowly associate of George M. Chamlin in West Long Branch, New Jersey. I jumped into the trenches of personal lawyering instead of establishment institutional activities.

At Rutgers, I was fortunate to train with some great teachers. Professors Kinoy, Knowlton, Brooks, Axelrod, Blumrosen, Mendlovitz and Heckel, along with my father, stimulated me to use my energies to cut through the morass of our legal bureaucracy, using our common law to achieve fairness and dignity for my clients. At times, I simply had to kick at it to make it work. At other times I needed–and still do–a bulldozer. I'm still kicking and where necessary, driving the dozer.

George had a small-town practice which handled closings, municipal court, small criminal matters and personal injury claims. Over the next twenty-five years we built our firm into Chamlin, Schottland, Rosen, Cavanaugh and Uliano with two offices and thirty-five employees. The firm got involved with numerous high visibility cases and became a significant player in the development of New Jersey common law.

In 1989, George and I had a falling out. It happens. We split the firm and I opened my own shop in Freehold, New Jersey. In 2005, I joined Lomurro, Davison, Eastman and Munoz which could and did provide me with the extra-ordinary support necessary to carry out my habit of taking cases appealing to me more from a justice standpoint than a monetary one.

In 2014, Don Lomurro withdrew the matrimonial and personal injury crew and we started Lomurro, Munson, Comer, Brown, and Schottland. I hope to end my career with this wonderful team.

What follows is my own legal odyssey, presented through a sampling of cases with which I have been associated, covering three time periods: The Early Years (1965-1980); The Middle Years (1980-2000); and The Twenty-First Century (2000-Present). I hope you enjoy reading the cases. I have enjoyed every battle.

My intent with this publication is a bit hazy. The result of taking approximately twenty-five years to write it all down. It started with a title of Trying for 25 Years and now morphed into a fifty-year story.

This is no overarching thesis. It is simply a play by play account of what I considered to be interesting stories. Each does however contain some personal editorial content, but I don't see one theme carrying through.

In each case, you be the judge as to how each case got presented, substantiated, or ultimately awarded a verdict.

MDS

The Early Years: 1965-1980

The Cribbing Case

The year after graduating from Rutgers, in the Spring of 1966, I was asked to represent two of four senior law students accused of cribbing on a final exam in tax law that Spring.

A dear friend was one of those accused. However, his family employed a senior partner of a well-respected Newark firm to represent him and one other of the accused. They admitted their cheating, and both lost a year, having to return and graduate the following year, in 1967. My clients insisted they were innocent, so four professors were empaneled to hear the case. The assistant dean acted as prosecutor and main witness; I had to cross-examine this man who only a year earlier, when I was a student, had held a dominant position of power over me.

This change in roles, though a little scary, freed and empowered me to use the skills against some of the very panel members who had taught them to me. My cross-examination revealed the assistant dean's allegations were based on mere hearsay and assumptions which could not stand as legal evidence. My clients were exonerated and allowed to graduate in 1966.

I don't believe there were other cases like this at Rutgers Law School before or since. The special panel applied a standard of reasonable doubt. A classroom ideal was turned into the raw reality of a trial. It was an exhilarating experience for me to participate in the transformation from theory to practice.

This was such a unique event it was recalled by one of the panel members at our 25th class reunion. He recounted the experience of seeing the concepts offered by him and his colleagues used in a real-life setting, at the very institution where those concepts had been taught. It was quite an eye opener for all of us. Sheer transformation.

From theory to practice.

Ladies and gentlemen start your engines!

Knapp v. Phillips Petroleum, 123 N.J. Super 26 (App. Div., 1973)

This 1973 major personal injury case arose out of a two-car vehicular collision occurring on Route 34 adjacent to a Phillips 66 gas station in Matawan, New Jersey.

I represented two passengers, Doris and George Beal, who were being driven to the airport by Doris's sister and brother-in-law, the Knapps. Beal had won a trip from American Motors for his salesmanship. Four Knapp children accompanied them on the trip to the airport.

An uninsured motorist, Wissing, had been traveling in the opposite direction and suddenly came onto the wrong side of the road, striking the Knapp vehicle head-on, killing one of the Knapp children and seriously injuring the other occupants. In the resulting lawsuit some of the most respected trial lawyers of the day were pitted against one another.

Louis Drazin, a legend at the Monmouth County trial bar, represented the Knapp family. Richard Amdur, who was to become the leading civil defense lawyer in New Jersey, represented Wissing and the U.C.J. – the Unsatisfied Claim and Judgement Fund. Robert Carton of the prestigious defense firm of Carton, Nary, Witt & Arvanitis represented Phillips Petroleum. The Carton firm was a third generation of leading and respected civil defense trial lawyers, Robert Carton being the dean of the group. Ralph Campbell, of the second leading defense firm in Monmouth County, Campbell, Mangini, Foley and Lee, represented the Knapps in defense of the Beals' affirmative claim, brought by me, the most unheralded of them all.

The Beals' claim had been referred to me by Drazin because of a possible conflict between the driver, Knapp, and the Beals.

The claims went to trial before Judge Walter Conklin and a jury. Judge Conklin was in the twilight of his judicial career, having been transferred from the Essex County Bench after many years of unspectacular service in the hub of New Jersey's calendar congestion, Essex County.

He had been transferred to Monmouth County in consideration for his faithful trial bench service and to allow him a shorter commute from his Pt. Pleasant home. A strong but colorless jurist, he surprised us all with his willingness to be fair, a trait far too many of his compatriots leave at home when driving to work each morning.

The claim against Wissing was simple: He had negligently come on the wrong side of the road. The theory against Phillips Petroleum was far more esoteric. Plaintiffs contended when Phillips constructed its gas station it had installed a "French Drain" diverting underground water toward and under

the abutting highway. When the water froze, it caused great concrete slabs to buckle and heave, resulting in the large hole Wissing claimed he sought to avoid by crossing over into the Knapps' lane of travel. Under the law Wissing, who was uninsured, was provided a defense by the U.C.J., which could pay a statutory maximum $30,000 toward a settlement, provided no other party was also found at fault.

The U.C.J., or "Fund" as it was called, was a weak mechanism adopted by the state legislature to provide minimum coverage for those involved in accidents with uninsured motorists. Because of the unreasonable evaluation techniques and miserly attitudes of its claims and administrative people, dealing with the Fund was a nightmare. Numerous uninsured motorist claims were tried even though there were certain provisions in the law-making adjudication impractical and unworkable.

By 1973, Fund cases had become the bane of trial judges and lawyers alike, contributing to a substantial portion of calendar backlog in New Jersey. It remained that way until the 1989/90 amendment to the No-Fault Law.

Settlement discussions were not fruitful. If no one else contributed, the Fund reluctantly offered its $30,000, a mere pittance, to split among all the plaintiffs. Phillips refused to offer one cent even though Drazin, as lead counsel, had offered to take $75,000 for the entire matter, including the Beals' claim. Once the trial began it became evident why he'd offered to take so little: He was surprisingly unprepared to prove a serious case against Phillips, though proof of Phillips' fault was the only way to secure more than $30,000 for the case.

All the plaintiffs had retained William Poznak, a civil engineer, to assist in the claim against Phillips. He opined that underground water from the Phillips property had contributed to creation of the hole. However, he had not done any real homework; hadn't reviewed the highway plans; hadn't done any test borings; hadn't reviewed the Phillips' plans prior to trial. Drazin installed me as the foil, requiring I go first with the Beals' claim.

I called Mr. Poznak to the stand. He was the single most important witness for the plaintiffs' claim, as his opinion was the linchpin for establishing any liability in Phillips. Yet none of us, me included, had bothered to direct him to secure the material necessary to support his bold opinion. Judge Conklin stopped my direct examination to give me and the witness a luncheon break to find the original Route 34 highway plans so Poznak would at least know the specifications for the concrete slabs broken up by the Phillips' water. We borrowed a car (which broke down during lunch) and managed to find the plans at the Department of Transportation field office on Route 9 in Howell Township, New Jersey. It was a hot day and my suit was drenched when Poznak resumed the stand. His theory now sounded scholarly and well-supported. Our good luck in finding the plans made me feel the outcome was predestined.

This journey was only the first of several Poznak and I made during trial recesses and over the weekend, piecing together the case against Phillips. Poznak drove to Philadelphia to purchase aerial shots of Route 34 made immediately prior to construction of the gas station. Sometimes we were weren't so lucky: The photos showed a bus going over the area of the hole, covering it.

The trial continued, highlighted by Philips' engineers caught trying to hide certain borings and using an obviously weak consulting engineer. In the last analysis, Judge Conklin's tolerance and even-handedness insured a fair trial for all and distinguished the entire proceeding.

After a long and arduous trial, the summations are great opportunities for well-spoken and fine-acting trial lawyers to put it all together for the jury. Bob Carton, who was giving his last civil jury summation, had two members of the jury yawning. At best, he angered the jury against his client, Phillips. Dick Amdur, who had nothing to lose, gave a succinct and at times hilarious summation, during which I had to control my own laughter. Next came the legend, Drazin. I waited with great expectation to see if he could bring tears to the eyes of the jurors.

He didn't. He was totally flat, unconcerned and uninspiring. He probably figured the Knapps were condemned to receive only the $30,000 Fund money. He even forgot to sum up for the deceased Knapp child.

My turn. I stepped forward, gave the omitted Knapp summation and, figuring I had nothing to lose, went after Phillips unmercifully. After two days of deliberations the jury returned a substantial six figure verdict against Phillips and Wissing. At the time, it was the largest civil verdict in Monmouth County.

Phillips took an appeal to the Superior Court Appellate Division. Its published opinion, affirming the verdict, is now part of the law regarding an abutting owner's liability for the effects of underground water on the public right of way.

I suffered two additional insults for my efforts. At oral argument of the appeal, Drazin's partner, Tom Warshaw, was afforded great deference by the court as the alter ego of the legend who had "secured" this great victory. The court merely tolerated me. Then came the final insult.

Under our financial arrangement, my fee would be one-third of the Beals' verdict. Their verdict of $25,000, a modest but fair one, yielded me $8,333. Obviously, if the Beal injuries had been more substantial, Drazin would have referred their case to one of the other leading lights of the plaintiffs' bar. Drazin's fee was substantially in excess of $200,000. Since I'd invested much more effort and contributed substantially to the ultimate result, I expected Drazin to offer me some token of his fee in appreciation.

What I received instead was his call saying he wasn't interested in receiving any of his customary referral fee. When I suggested he acknowledge my contribution with a small portion of the overall fee, his response was "don't be silly." My senior partner, a former associate of Louis Drazin, had warned me not to expect what I felt was owed. He was right and I was wrong.

In retrospect, while disappointed in Drazin's efforts during the trial and the financial aftermath, I did appreciate the opportunity to try such an important case so early in my career. Drazin underwrote large expenses for preparation and trial of the matter, was cordial to work with and helped me grow as a trial attorney. I came to understand legends don't always perform up to their reputations. While true in this case, the trial was a great learning experience for me in many ways.

Whenever I see Bill Poznak, we talk like a couple of kids who jointly engineered entrance to the cookie jar. Perhaps we did. Also, I became great friends with Drazin's sons who took over their dad's fine practice.

This case was a watershed case for all of the lawyers. Robert Carton and Ralph Campbell never tried another jury trial. Richard Amdur went on to become a top defense lawyer, especially in medical malpractice cases and at age 80 was still trying cases. I too was propelled forward to my extensive and multi-faceted career.

Doe v. County of Monmouth: My First Million Dollar Award

[The client's actual name has been deleted as the case was not a reported opinion and I wish to protect her privacy.]

I had a friend who was well-respected, a husband, father of four children, a leading urologist/surgeon and a deeply religious man. He lived and worked in Long Branch.

On his trip home from his office near Monmouth Medical Center, he usually drove the back way over a narrow bridge into the Elberon area. One cold winter night, planning to go home and change into his tennis gear to go get some exercise, he never made it home. For reasons which will never be fully understood, he drove his new Jaguar into a guardrail which failed, flipping him and his vehicle into about four feet of water and mud. He was found dead.

I was away at the time. Scanning the accumulated newspapers on my return, I discovered the front-page story of his horrible death. His widow asked our firm to block an autopsy since it was against Orthodox belief. Judge Lawrence Stamelman signed an order to protect the family and the soul of my client from that final insult.

His widow and I discussed the known facts and possible explanations for how her husband, who knew the area so well, could have driven into the guardrail and suffered this terrible accident.

There were various explanations, some plausible, some not. I undertook an investigation to determine the causes of what had occurred and to evaluate the significance of the remaining evidence. The starting point was the vehicle which we'd placed in storage at a garage in Hazlet, N.J. Experts examined the vehicle and tires. We were unable to establish any vehicular failure; however, we did discover a significant piece of evidence.

Wedged into the right front suspension system was a 4" x 4" piece of wood which came from the base of the bridge rail. My investigator removed the piece and we went to the scene, discovering exactly where it had broken off. This began an extensive accident reconstruction which would involve one of the foremost forensic experts in the country. Using some of the most modern and sophisticated technology, we were able to reconstruct the path of travel, speed and attitude of the vehicle from initial impact with the approach guardrail until the final resting place in the mud and water below.

We then analyzed the components of the structure with which the vehicle made contact. The purpose of the bridge guardrail system was simply to keep a vehicle on the bridge, not to provide a system of hazardous roadblocks for vehicles in trouble. Our analysis revealed the structure was very unsound and unsuited as the emergency system for which it was designed.

Monmouth County was responsible for maintaining the system of bridges within the county on all roads except state highways. The bridge department had installed flex beam approach rails but failed to connect them to the bridge rail, creating the possibility of a double failure. First, the approach rail would not take a direct hit from an automobile without coming down, offering no impediment to the vehicle continuing off the embankment into the water below. Second, if the initial impact was a glancing blow, the structure would direct the vehicle to the unattached bridge rail which, because of its independent status, became a serious obstruction for the vehicle. The combination of these two glaring inadequacies caused my client's death.

We concluded he had driven the vehicle into the approach rail on an obtuse trajectory. As that rail came down, it directed his vehicle into the post and end of the bridge rail which, itself, came apart at impact. That rail lifted up and caused the vehicle to travel along the side of the bridge, half on and half off, until the rear pivoted, and the car flipped over and off the bridge into a watery grave.

It was my opinion that the county was negligent and could be held liable for my client's untimely and grisly death, so I instituted suit on behalf of his estate and dependents. The defense contended my client had been negligent and speeding. It also invoked what are known as Title 59 (Public Entity Liability) defenses.

It has been the subject of considerable controversy over the years. The body of common law began with a general immunity, but as notions of liability changed over the years, that immunity eroded until the New Jersey Supreme Court essentially struck it away. The legislature, fearful the state and its various subdivisions and agencies would be over-burdened as the result of the negligence of its agents, passed a detailed and confusing law providing a middle ground between full liability and total immunity.

The law provided for immunity where the decision on how a project or bridge would be erected was formally approved by a local legislative body such as a town council or planning board. However, where the plan was set up by an agent, such as a road foreman, no immunity was afforded.

Likewise, if a condition of governmental property was improper or dangerous, the public entity could argue it didn't have adequate funding to correct that condition.

Claims like my clients were fraught with uncertainty and legal pitfalls and Title 59 defenses.

In preparing this case we did get extremely lucky. Eighteen months before the fatal accident the county had received a report from an independent consulting firm indicating this exact approach and bridge guardrail system was incapable of taking a load and retaining its integrity. The report complained of the very things our experts had pointed out. This fact and the county's inaction by simply ignoring the report enhanced our case considerably.

Perhaps the most shocking feature of the whole affair was the county's response to the accident and claim. The day following the accident, the bridge department restored the entire system as it was the day before the accident. When I questioned the chief county engineer during deposition, his position was the county couldn't afford to correct the unsafe condition, contending the Woodgate Avenue Bridge and its approach rail was simply one of numerous defects in the county bridge system. They declined to try to correct the problem; instead, due to allegedly limited resources, opted to fix only the most acute and dangerous condition, even though our expert had opined it could be considerably strengthened spending only a few hundred dollars per connection.

Our case then settled. Following that settlement, the newspapers discovered how the experts had all complained of the same problem. After interviewing county representatives, they published a long expose'.

In settling this claim for a substantial sum, the insurance company also opted not to ensure it wouldn't happen again. It could have insisted the county correct the system. It did not because most insurers are not set up to do that–they just defend against and pay claims.

The next time you think about the high cost of liability insurance, remember that little bridge in Elberon, and all these little bridges everywhere waiting for another vehicle. Think of county bridge departments and county engineers not caring, and insurance companies which simply pay and pass that cost on. Isn't anyone listening? Doesn't anyone care? Is it all some fantasy? For the widow and her four children it was a nightmare.

The claim was paid. The children became adults. The mother has gone on with her life. Finally, more than five years after the settlement, the county replaced the defective guard rail system. Five years.

Individually, this was my first civil claim of more than a million dollars. Success came through thorough investigation, good expert support, and a bit of good luck.

Doe v. Spantex
(1982)

This case with an international flavor arose out of the crash of a DC-10 off the runway at Malaga, Spain. My client was a passenger on an overloaded flight of tourists preparing to return to Madrid and then on home to the U.S.A.

It was apparent the people running the airline, in an effort to maximize profits, were determined to get as many people and as much baggage onto the craft as possible. Unfortunately, the load exceeded the limit of a DC-10 at the altitude of that airport. Airports around the world, which are above sea level, require a proportionate reduction in on board fuel to permit a successful lift off.

In Malaga, they had filled the fuel supply to capacity by mistake, causing a loss of the required necessary lift.[1] The DC-10 could not achieve an adequate lift speed. Though the pilot aborted the takeoff, he ran out of runway. The craft crossed onto a major highway, striking a bridge abutment and catching fire. Panic ensued and the passengers and crew fled as the mighty aircraft, along with about seventy human beings, was reduced to ashes.

My client, one of the fortunate ones, got out before the fire turned into a holocaust but still suffered second and third degree

---

[1] I personally discovered this is common in other airports, such as Johannesburg in South Africa, where on my flight home they had to stop and refill because they remembered the airport was 6,000 feet above sea level and a full 747 could take off with only half a tank.

burns on her face, shoulder and arm. In taking this case, I got quite an education on disaster litigation.

Every time there was an aircraft disaster, lawyers who considered themselves specialists worked with agents who went to the scene and combed the hospitals for clients. They contacted the families of the injured and deceased and ran as many claims as they could to maximize their earnings.

The plaintiff, who had been a client of mine before the misfortune, was contacted by these unscrupulous charlatans at the hospital in Spain and again after her return to New Jersey. They freely bragged of their expertise and denigrated me and other attorneys.

When there is a common disaster like a plane crash or claims with a common thread of liability such as the Dalkon Shield (IUD) cases, litigation is controlled through a series of rules seeking to centralize discovery and dispose of the multiple claims. This multi-district litigation technique is a good idea in theory. In practice it has become a haven for "specialists" to get the coveted appointment to the "Committee."

Committee members are, of course, attorneys who have established a relationship with the plaintiffs. But not all the attorneys are appointed to the Committee. Appointments are made by the Federal Judge to whom the matter is assigned. This results in whopping legal fees to committee members - a percentage of the gross awards made to all the claimants. The defendants' agents are required to make a direct payment of the fees from the damage awards. While the percentages are low, the gross amounts are substantial due to the nature of the claims and the number of claimants.

As an interested observer, I attended two court meetings of the multi-district people in connection with the Malaga, Spain disaster. What a shock to see these "experts" argue, fight and bray, jockeying for position and securing that coveted appointment to the Plaintiffs' Lawyers Committee.

The big question in this matter was whether the treaty limiting the amount of recovery for international air disasters was applicable[2]. Members of the committee and several other lawyers knew that in this case defendants would not be able to avail themselves of that limitation because of all things, the print size on the ticket terms and conditions stating the limit was smaller than required by law, as established in a published opinion of the Second Circuit Court of Appeals.

The liability issue itself was rather mundane and presented no great problem for any experienced plaintiffs' litigator. [That Second Circuit opinion was later reversed by our U.S. Supreme Court, though it did not affect Spantex.]

Several well-known law firms sought appointment to the Committee, knowing such appointment was a seven-figure-plus-fee guarantee for work which could be done by relatively low-paid associates. A real revered bonanza.

Preparation of the cases meant completing depositions of the surviving claimants and obtaining the necessary exchange of information, medical examinations and reports common to personal injury claims. I settled the claim for what I considered twice its value. My fee was limited by the strict court rule then in effect in New Jersey. It had been suggested to me I refer my client's claim to certain New York counsel so we could secure a contingent fee more like 50°/o of the recovery. I declined the invitation, but still suffered the loss of a substantial portion of my fee to the Plaintiff's Committee which simply had to secure appointment to earn it. No heavy lifting on their part was required.

When the Committee moved to have the fee approved as a piece of each case, I wrote the court, expressing my belief—and the real fact— that the Committee's work and expertise was unnecessary. As you could expect, my objection was ignored, and

---

[2]The Warsaw Treaty with the Montreal Protocol called for a payment limit of less than $100,000 at the time.

the Committee split up millions of dollars in legal fees, probably averaging several thousand dollars an hour. Shameful!

Some governmental authority should examine what goes on with these air crash cases and multi-district litigation personal injury matters. They are subject to great abuse by the self-proclaimed "lawyer experts." Really, what the attorneys are expert at is sweeping up clients and figuring angles to increase their fees. Judges appear to think this is all a legitimate part of the game. I got educated. Maybe the public should be let in on this dirty little secret.

My client's claim included her fear of flying. When her settlement check came in and I needed her signature, I had to wait until she returned from abroad via a 747: She had gotten the last laugh.

State v. Vinegra 134 N.J. Super 432 (App. Div., 1975) aff'd 73 N.J. 484 (1977)

Victor Vinegra was the city engineer of Elizabeth, and no stranger to the whims of county and municipal politics. Still, he was more than a little surprised to be hauled before the Grand Jury by an ambitious prosecutor of Union County who, without advising him of his rights or that he was a suspect or "target", as they call it, asked Vinegra questions about a road building project. Without any evidence of wrongdoing other than mere suspicion, the prosecutor secured an indictment based on Vinegra's testimony. The indictment alleged a whole series of acts of misconduct by Vinegra without any direct evidence other than vague allegations of failure to properly supervise the construction and some cost overruns.

To the credit of the Mayor of the City of Elizabeth, notwithstanding the indictment, Vinegra was not suspended and stayed on the job while the case was litigated through to the New Jersey Supreme Court.

I was retained to represent Vinegra in defense of the criminal charges. Under our Constitution, specifically the Fifth Amendment, a body of law has developed forbidding a prosecutor from "hauling" in a target before Grand Jury investigation without giving him the appropriate warnings of his rights. In addition, at the time, New Jersey had a specific law granting immunity for testimony of public officials subpoenaed to testify before a Grand Jury, provided the witness requested it. Based on that law and the violation of Vinegra's Fifth Amendment rights, we filed a motion to dismiss the indictment. The motion was heard before Judge James Coleman, Jr., Superior Court judge in Elizabeth, New Jersey.

After a careful review of the matter, Judge Coleman decided Vinegra's rights had been violated and that violation tainted the indictment. He therefore ordered the indictment dismissed.

The State appealed to the Superior Court, Appellate Division. The issue: was the misconduct of the Union County Prosecutor of such nature to warrant dismissal of the entire indictment or did the statute simply immunize Vinegra from use of his own testimony at the trial. The Appellate Division ruled the State could not use Vinegra's testimony against him but that Counts 1-7 of the indictment could be restored for trial.

Both the State and defense took the matter to the state Supreme Court. In a 5-2 opinion, the court affirmed the action of the Appellate Division in sending the matter back for trial, but ruled the State had the burden of persuading a trial judge that prior to trial the evidence intended to be used against Vinegra was not obtained as a direct or indirect result of his testimony, which had been wrongfully compelled before the Grand Jury. I am certain the majority opinion did not realize they were essentially ending the case against Victor Vinegra.

There was no way that the Union County Prosecutor could establish the entire scenario sought to be proven against Vinegra was obtained any other way than directly or indirectly through his "spilling the beans" before the Grand Jury.

This case was a landmark in the "use immunity" concept in New Jersey; the two dissents are possibly the longest ever written in the history of N.J. jurisprudence[3]. These dissents, which went further than the majority opinion in immunizing officials who, like Vinegra, had their rights violated, may be the most thorough and

[3] Chief Justice Hughes and Justice Pashman wrote this distinguished dissent.

comprehensive review of our Grand Jury system and the standard which should to be imposed against prosecutors.

Regardless of the Supreme Court's ruling sending the case back for trial, the practical impact of providing protection from the taint of illegally obtained evidence put the Union County Prosecutor in an impossible situation. He recognized that situation and took a dismissal of the indictment, without trial. I'll never forget the call I received from the assistant prosecutor advising that they were dismissing the indictment.

Judge Coleman, starting as a workers' compensation judge, was the first man of color to serve on the Supreme Court, now retired. He had the nerve to take on a powerful prosecutor; his action was a rare example of a judge putting a check on an overzealous prosecutor.

State v. Blanton, 166 N.J. Super 62 (App. Div., 1979)

The north end of Long Branch, New Jersey is primarily a low-income, black section. With good reason, the police department tries to avoid confrontations in that area. Mr. Elijah Blanton, a large black man, then of sixty years or so, lived in the north end. He had been the gardener for a former Attorney General of New Jersey. Elijah was one of the strongest persons I have ever met and had the arms and hands of a giant.

I first met Elijah when asked to defend his son, Frank, who was charged along with Elijah for assaulting police officers in a fracas near Elijah's home. During that melee, Elijah had lifted and tossed the largest member of the police department, a man 6'6" tall and 240 pounds, like a child's doll.

Elijah was convicted, but his son was acquitted.

That incident spawned a legend. When Elijah, an otherwise gentle man, saw the police, it was like waving the color red at a bull.

A few years later, on a hot summer night, several black kids were causing a disturbance near Elijah's home. Someone made the mistake of calling the police. When they arrived, several cars strong, Elijah was on the adjoining playground trying to restore order. Because of his reputation, he was singled out by the police. There followed an attempt by several Long Branch officers to arrest and handcuff the elder Blanton.

Also present on the playground was one of Elijah's athletic sons, John Blanton. He was a recent graduate of Long Branch

High School and about to attend college on a track scholarship. When John saw the officers battling with his father, he is alleged to have thrown something at an officer, striking the officer's head. The officer suffered a relatively serious head injury. John denied doing it but attempted to run when the police tried to arrest him.

Formal, serious criminal charges were brought against both Elijah and John. Typical for trials of the time a white jury convicted the two defendants. They were scheduled to be sentenced when John was already into his second year at college. With his record of prior confrontations with police, Elijah expected and did receive incarceration for his participation in the unfortunate incident.

John, the first of the family to try to escape the black ghetto by attending college, hoped the sentencing judge would recognize the incident resulted from an extreme situation which would not occur again. The trial judge, demonstrating insensibility, insensitivity and racial bias sentenced young John to the Youth Correction Center for a term of approximately fourteen months.

This sentence, if carried out, meant the end of his effort to escape the ghetto cycle. We requested the judge stay the sentence pending appeal. This was denied and it became necessary to make an emergent application to an Appellate Division judge. That individual grasped the need for immediate relief and granted bail pending appeal. That was an unusual event–rare actually–bail pending appeal in a case where a black defendant was appealing a conviction for assaulting a white police officer.

Ultimately, the full Appellate court reversed the sentence and directed John be placed on probation. That opinion was published and the trial judge publicly criticized for his lack of judgment and insight. The final chapter was written when the Sports Section of the Star Ledger ran an article with a picture of John Blanton, describing his success coaching a Newark girls' basketball team.

Fortunately, John was not tarnished or burned by this close call with another mindless trial judge. Many are not as fortunate.

Our criminal justice system has been jaded by the avalanche of cases, claims and appeals brought about with the advent of the Public Defender system. It took one hundred seventy-five years for the U.S. Supreme Court, in Gideon v. Wainwright 372 U.S. 335 (1963), to hold that defendants in criminal cases are entitled to a lawyer at public expense through certain critical phases of a criminal matter. Meantime, our system has been engulfed by a virtual avalanche of what are perceived as groundless appeals. Check the statistics and the racial make-ups of our jails. Bias is rampant.

The Blanton case finalized in 1979; during the 2016 Presidential election campaign, the one thing all candidates seemed to agree on was that the criminal justice system is broken, as evidenced by the high incidence of black incarceration. Thirty-seven years and *no* change speaks volumes about the "system".

Many of our judges have simply circled the wagons and adopted a siege mentality, resulting in a loss of both spontaneity and fairness. Judges generally have an excellent feel or intuitive sense on a given question. In the criminal law field, much of this has been lost, replaced instead by some need to do what the judge believes that the public expects. The corresponding loss of humanity and empathy for a person or set of circumstances leaves people like John Blanton subject to political abuse under the guise of judges "just following the law." Fortunately for John, a somewhat enlightened and brave panel of the Appellate Division heard his appeal.

The numbers of arrests generated from strict enforcement of so many laws has turned judges off; they don't listen and can no longer separate the bona fide from nonsense. The overall quality of defense has gone down and there are far fewer creative defense arguments and far more judicial rubber-stamped sentences. The numbers are so overwhelming that the system is breaking down. More stringent laws require more jail sentences, yet we are insensitive to the need to provide both adequate representation and reasonable alternatives to incarceration. If we do not see some real leadership on this issue, our society is in for continuous and growing trouble.

Our current criminal justice system is not color blind and even with a black president, our leaders have been unable to stop the injustice heaped on the minorities by police and prosecutors. The Public Defender system, so needed for so long, has been no match for the onslaught, yet receives very little help from our judges. The entire system is riddled with racism and intolerance.

The Chelsea School Case: Long Branch Division of Taxpayers v. Cowan and City of Long Branch, 199 N.J. Super 30 (App. Div., 1972)

The City of Long Branch in Monmouth County, New Jersey is a shore community. In years gone by it was a famous summer vacation spot of the rich and famous, including presidents. By the 1970s and 80s its main claim to fame was the "Haunted Mansion" on the great fishing pier. A fire destroyed that!

Following World War II, Long Branch had a very large Catholic community with a private Catholic school known as the Star of the Sea Academy. The Academy, located on Chelsea Avenue, a block and a half from the ocean, was run by the Sisters of Charity.

By the early 1970s the school was falling into disrepair with much of the land and buildings sitting idle. The Sisters were concerned with the accompanying financial drain. However, in Trenton was a friendly governor who had within his executive departments, people who could serve both the public interest as well as the interests of the Sisters of Charity. The idea, attractive to many in the Department of Health, was to purchase the land and the run-down facility from the Sisters, then invest several million dollars to rehabilitate the buildings and use them as a residential center for drug rehabilitation, an investment that would also rehabilitate the Sisters' treasury.

An entire staff could be employed to house and retain adolescents and young adults who were mired in some form of drug dependence.

Governor Cahill, a Catholic, asked for two land appraisals, one by the county Democratic leader and one by the Republican county leader, both of whom were also Catholic. The Governor then asked the Department of Health to begin the necessary steps to set up the program. When the local community got wind of the nature of the intended use, the outrage of this use quickly erupted.

While the community wanted to help the Sisters of Charity out of their dilemma to unload this white elephant, they were fiercely opposed to bringing hundreds of drug-dependent young people into an already drug- troubled area. Both legal and political assaults were mounted in opposition to this effort. I was retained by a local association to institute legal action to try to halt this local neighborhood invasion.

The case was instituted in the Chancery Division of the Superior Court, Monmouth County. The City of Long Branch joined in the claim against the Department of Health, claiming the decision to locate the Center at the abandoned school was illogical, arbitrary and unreasonable. The office of the State Attorney General came in to defend the action on behalf of the state officials. I was quickly faced with a motion to dismiss my case–the defense claiming that even if one accepted everything in the complaint, as true it did not justify stopping or halting the project.

The Chancery Division judge was the Honorable M. Raymond McGowan who himself was a member of the Catholic faith. After indulging my argument for about ten minutes; he threw me out on my ear.

"Here we go again," I said to myself.

So, I filed an appeal. At oral argument in the Appellate Division, I discovered a beneficent attitude. Sure enough, they issued an opinion, since published, recognizing that my complaint did state a claim. They directed a full hearing. On remand the case was referred by Judge McGowan to his "fellow" Catholic, Judge Francis X. Crahay for trial. It was done so quickly I was not even permitted any discovery. I couldn't get the records I needed, nor the depositions of people who knew the underlying administrative facts. But at least they did give us a hearing. The appearance of fairness was all we could obtain.

We all went down to the site and inspected the grounds and facility. Sure enough, it was a run-down dump in a nice middle-class neighborhood in Long Branch. I remember walking through it and thinking of the Catacombs of Rome. The State was on rather thin ice, seeking to justify the large expenditure of funds needed to rehabilitate and modernize the place.

Looking to avoid the religion angle of the case and the "how could you not want to help the Sisters" aspect, we brought in a leading land-use expert who mopped the floor with the Attorney General. In the end, of course, Judge Crahay issued a crisp opinion, saying all the right things and making all the necessary findings so a reviewing court would not upset the opinion.

Judge Crahay did what Judge McGowan hadn't done: made it look and sound right. But, although the deck had been stacked against the local claim from the very first, at last we had made them sit up and take notice.

We lost the battle, but in the end, won the war. The Sisters of Charity got their bailout. The State changed the intensity of its commitment and never fully spent the money to make it a full-blown residential drug rehabilitation center. Instead, they scaled the project way down, choosing it as a day school for youths with drug-related problems. At any one time they never had more than 50-75 students at the facility, and it never became the show place first intended.

Millions of tax dollars were saved. The community did not suffer, and Governor Cahill escaped review of his actions. In a stroke of irony, the same Judge Crahay presided at the criminal trial of Governor Cahill's Secretary of State, Paul Sherwin. And as an ultimate quirk of fate, Judge Crahay's law secretary, Tom Cavanagh, also a Catholic, became a member of my firm and a partner. He later joined the bench in Monmouth County and became Chancery Division judge (Retired) like his former master, Judge Crahay. Amazing, is it not?

I took the case knowing it could not be won, but it was interesting watching the system struggle with itself to determine how fair it should be with us. If I'd made a direct attack on the Governor or the Catholic issue in the pleadings, the establishment wouldn't even have given us a hearing. Because we were nice, they were nice and at least they made it look nice. Once again, the trial judges did what they thought was expected of them by their superiors.

There is a class of cases creating extreme anxiety for the brethren of the Bench. This one was a classic!

It is a rare pleasure of the practice to watch judges struggle to deny a legitimate case and appear to be doing it fairly. They brought in two of their best to smooth it over: Morton Greenberg, Esq., Assistant Attorney General, as trial counsel who has now become a judge of the Third Circuit Court of Appeals (retired), and Francis X. Crahay, Esq., trial judge, who was subsequently elevated to the Superior Court Appellate Division and ultimately retired. What a team play. In the final irony, the State ultimately closed the place, which remained vacant and abandoned for many years until finally disposed of. It is still a non-event on Chelsea Avenue in Long Branch.

Until Justice Scalia's death, six of the nine U.S. Supreme Court members were Catholics. At present there are only three non-Catholics sitting on our Supreme Court so Catholics control the legal heartbeat of our land.

Quite something to consider.

The State Trooper Case: Manzo Contracting

This was a dilly of a case, and how I got it is almost as interesting as the case itself.

In 1968, my first wife was in labor with our second child. We lived in Freehold and the hospital was in Neptune, New Jersey, about twelve miles to the east.

It began at the Freehold Circle where we ran into traffic. A trooper was directing traffic at the location and with the imminent threat of an in-vehicle birth, I asked if we could cut ahead of some vehicles. The officer understood our plight and volunteered to provide an escort to the hospital.

He activated his dome lights and led me through the Route 33 traffic at speeds between 60 and 90 m.p.h. We arrived at the hospital with about ten minutes to spare. I had a chance to talk to the officer and discovered he'd had a rather severe accident several months before.

It turned out, that while on routine patrol on Route 33 West of Freehold he had seen a car pass a stop sign while making a right turn onto Route 33. He took up pursuit and the vehicle accelerated onto a portion of the roadway that was in the process of being dualized by the Manzo Contracting Company. While in pursuit, he did a look-up on the plate; the owner was wanted for armed robbery. The vehicle had two occupants and appeared to be trying to elude the officer at double the speed limit.

As they entered the construction area, the troop car got abreast of the suspects' vehicle which lurched to the left, striking the trooper's vehicle at the passenger side rear. This maneuver caused the fleeing vehicle to spin and run off the road toward the center median strip, run up a large pile of sand, catapult through the air and come down directly on top of a Manzo Contracting Co. tractor left on the median strip behind the pile of sand. The impact killed the two occupants instantly.

Meanwhile, the trooper fought to retain control after being struck by the suspects' car. His vehicle started to fishtail, skid and slide violently as he'd been traveling at 100 m.p.h. at initial impact. The trooper desperately steered toward the skid, aiming his vehicle for an area of the median strip which he thought safe. Unfortunately, that same tractor blocked his path and the vehicle ran directly into it, bringing the chase to a sudden and violent end.

My client was lucky to survive the impact with a stationary tractor probably two and one-half times the weight of the troop car. Knowing this time that I was on the side of the good guy, I took his case and sued the Manzo Contracting Company for negligently leaving an unlit tractor on a median strip on a public roadway where it could present a hazard for a vehicle in an emergency. Some of my fellow lawyers thought I would be laughed out of court with that claim. The trooper and I suspected the court would be more tolerant of our case; which it was.

The court refused a motion to dismiss and the case was submitted, with a wink, to a jury for its determination. Notwithstanding a fine effort by the defense claiming there was nothing wrong with leaving a tractor on the median during the construction of a highway, I thought I saw the foreman of the jury wink himself when he delivered the verdict in favor of my client. Manzo had been negligent.

The defendant was so shocked with the verdict, it appealed to the Superior Court, Appellate Division, arguing it was ridiculous to conclude they'd been negligent for simply parking the tractor on the median off the travelled portion of the roadway when that tractor was being used in the construction. One didn't expect to encounter vehicles traveling 100 m.p.h. in a construction zone. These were valid and compelling arguments countered by a simply more compelling fact: The trooper was doing the business of the King, the New Jersey State Police, when injured. The deceased was operating an uninsured vehicle and his estate was virtually penniless. Myopia set in and the trooper declared the winner.

It was oddly wonderful to be on this side and so persuasive with our learned jurists. How sweet it was to have everyone (except the defendant) rooting for us.

The contrast between the Cribbing Case and the State Trooper case is almost chilling. The panel of law school professors showed a true commitment to concepts of "due process" and "reasonable doubt". The judges connected to the State Trooper case showed a true commitment to the status of the parties before them. This was the truism emerging from these cases. When the trial courts and our Appellate courts are confronted with cases which could upset political correctness of the time or political wishes of the establishment, they bend justice to suit the status quo or political threat. In my career, I have seen this happen again and again. In the State Trooper case, I happened to be on the side of the establishment.

The next case illustrates what happens when you're on the other side of the equation.

State v. A. and A. v. Sisco

These two trials, involving the same client, arose from one incident. They provide a stark lesson on how judicial action can sway the outcome.

The story begins at a rest area on the New Jersey Turnpike. Three young people had stopped their car in an off-limits section of the area. My client was the back-seat passenger in a properly licensed and registered New York vehicle.

Onto the scene came State Trooper Frannie Sisco, who was blessed with one of the keenest olfactory senses on the entire force. He determined these three had been engaging in the major offense of smoking grass or hash at some point earlier in the day. He ordered the youths (pronounced "yutes")[4] from the car and while they stood to the rear, conducted a search uncovering some suspected marijuana residue and a half dozen joints. As he returned to his troop car to radio for back-up, the young men, sensing they were in for trouble, climbed back into their vehicle and departed the scene. There followed a highspeed chase rivaling any Hollywood chase sequence.

At a deposition, Trooper Sisco admitted to firing over three dozen rounds from his .38 revolver at the fleeing vehicle and exceeding speeds of 90 miles per hour on our public highways. The chase continued from the Turnpike to the Raritan Bridge, to Route 9 in Sayreville, ultimately ending at a bridge abutment in Manalapan Township, Monmouth County, New Jersey.

---

[4] See "My Cousin Vinnie"

At least two other police departments, Marlboro and Sayreville, joined in the chase. Though they didn't know why the trooper was in pursuit, they still discharged firearms at the fleeing vehicle.

A member of the Marlboro Township Police Department was at the roadside near Route 9 as the vehicles approached. He aimed his trusty .357 Magnum at the right rear tire of the vehicle, fired and missed the tire.

Instead, the bullet went through the passenger side of the vehicle, striking A in the leg and exiting the vehicle on the driver's side. Shortly after this flagrant act, one of the bullets from Sisco's .38 passed through the skull of the driver, splattering his brains all over the front windshield. So it was that these three fugitives were brought to justice.

The Middlesex County Prosecutor secured an indictment of A. for escape and possession of marijuana. A duly convened Monmouth County Grand Jury cleared the trooper of any criminal charges regarding his conduct in killing the driver. I was retained to defend A. and pursue an action for his injuries.

One of my very first acts was to obtain copies of the grand jury investigation in Middlesex County by getting the permission of the criminal assignment judge in that county. I then asked his permission to obtain the records of the Monmouth County Grand Jury.

The court declined, stating I needed the permission of the Monmouth County criminal assignment judge. I promptly made a request to that Honorable Sir but was told since this was a charge arising in Middlesex, I needed to get an order from that vicinage.

Now I had two learned jurists pointing at each other to give the okay; a matter for determination by our Appellate Division. An appeal such as this is interlocutory in nature, requiring permission of the court to which appeal is sought. Not all that concerned with dispensing justice, the Appellate court declined my leave to appeal and left me with no access to obtain those records.

The procedural efforts to block my proper defense of the case were extreme, but I doggedly took the long shot and filed a motion with our State Supreme Court asking special permission to review those conflicting views and just maybe get to the bottom of what happened before the Monmouth County Grand Jury. All I wanted was access to a transcript of testimony of witnesses before the Grand Jury. Since those proceedings are secret, it's necessary to get a court order to obtain the transcripts.

One Friday morning I received two interesting telephone calls. The first came from the Clerk of the Supreme Court. He told me to appear the following Monday to argue my motion to the Supreme Court. The second was from my friend at the Monmouth County Prosecutor's office. His call was even more intriguing. It went something like this:

"Hey Mike, guess who just called?"

I had no idea.

"Well," he said, "the Chief Justice of the New Jersey Supreme Court, Joe Weintraub himself. And he was asking me about our motion. He asked if I would appear Monday to discuss the details. He said he had some questions. One had to do with what was in the transcripts of the hearing. I told him he would have to get that from the prosecutor who'd presented the matter. I then transferred his call."

As I then expected, I blandly watched our State Supreme Court go through every appearance of fairness that following Monday. Shortly after, I received the transcripts which told me absolutely nothing new except to confirm a whitewash had been done for Trooper Sisco. Obviously, the court wanted to satisfy itself of the condition of the record before I received access. Having been assured there was nothing of value, the court benevolently granted my motion.

Off we went to New Brunswick to defend the criminal case against my client. It turned out somebody in our government had lost the evidence (marijuana) so that count was speedily dismissed. The trial judge, sensing the gravity of what had occurred, acquitted A. on the escape charge at the end of the State's case. That was a judge properly doing his job, regardless of the consequences.

The criminal charges had been ludicrous to begin with. However, agents of our government thought nothing of putting this individual through the anxiety and expense of defending against them. The prefix "Grand" has nothing to do with the quality of work done by, or the independence of, the public bodies known as the Grand Jury. Mostly, it does the handiwork of the Prosecutor.

I began to have hopes my patience would pay off and actual justice might be available in our Federal Civil Rights claim against the various police officers involved in the shooting. Then I learned which federal judge had been assigned the case: none other than that famous, former federal prosecutor, the Honorable Fred Lacey.

Lacey was a man who could be depended on to protect and preserve the Constitution—as he interpreted it—like none before him. I had as much chance with him for an open-minded and fair consideration of this case as with the Marlboro Chief of Police or the detective who conducted the internal state police investigation.

The preparation and trial before Judge Lacey proved his reputation. We were forced to waste considerable time sitting around Newark, and eventually treated to his strong convictions against civil rights cases like these. However, the longest delay and insult to justice was occasioned not by Judge Lacey but of all people, my own client.

One fine spring morning I received a call from a Major Logan who had done the internal investigation of the incident for New Jersey's finest. After identifying himself, he started to laugh, advising me that subsequent to the shooting, my client-victim had been arrested and convicted in Elmira, New York for armed robbery of a bank taking place about three months prior to our incident. Talk about letting the air out of my balloon. We had to wait for his release from jail to move the case.

It was obvious that his conviction for that serious crime (albeit his first) would not sit well with a jury. Though, according to law, his conviction could only be used to affect credibility; as a practical matter it turned him from a victim into a serious lawbreaker.

Even if I prevailed on the question of liability, any damage award would be greatly reduced. After battling with Judge Lacey when we finally came to trial (our case consolidated with that of the driver's estate), we had no more stomach for the case and accepted a pittance of a settlement. Maybe, having come full circle, it was best to end the tragedy in that fashion. I had finally been worn down and exhausted by all the nonsense.

I am not proud of the result, but it sometimes gets very lonely out there without any help or support from the client. We are taught we will be subjected to fair treatment by our courts, that great bastion of liberty and fairness. Apparently, though, not all of the time and not for all of the people.

The judge in the criminal case had treated us and the case in a fair manner. The federal judge in Newark was 180 degrees the opposite, letting his personal bias trump an even-handed treatment of our claim. A biased judge forced both the driver's estate and my client to accept peanuts for death, serious injuries, and the terrible events.

Incidentally and yes, ironically, shortly after the case concluded, Trooper Sisco was promoted to sergeant.

The case certainly had a wild bunch of characters: a trigger-happy State Trooper, a corrupt Chief Justice, and a criminal client.

What a journey! What a potpourri of currents.

State v. G. and State v. S.

These cases were what is known as "death-by-auto" or "vehicular homicide" trials. In both, the driving appeared egregious, yet the defendants were acquitted. I have included them to illustrate examples of how juries, when not interfered with by an over-controlling trial judge, reach the right result on the evidence as presented. Juries will follow the evidence regardless of where it leads, provided the trial judge leaves them to their job.

STATE v. G.

Joseph G. was a young man driving a vehicle over the Thomas A. Mathis Bridge on Route 37 from Seaside Heights to Toms River. After spending the evening on the boardwalk, he was proceeding westerly alone in his car. Directly ahead of him on the bridge was a motorcycle with a 20-year-old male operator and a 19-year-old female companion. For some inexplicable reason, the vehicle ran up on the motorcycle, striking it from behind, knocking the two riders to the pavement and driving over the body of the female companion.

The vehicle then continued over the bridge, turned around and drove back in the wrong lane, almost striking the victims a second time before coming to a halt. Though the motorcycle operator survived, the young lady died from injuries sustained in the accident.

My client was charged with several crimes including vehicular homicide. My investigator, who was assigned to obtain statements from the witnesses (and there were many) suggested we desist because of the uniformly unhelpful nature of their observations. I insisted we go forward and obtain written statements from them all.

The incident was investigated by the Dover Township Police Department with the arresting officer insistent on taking samples of J.G.'s blood. The test result indicated a level of blood alcohol well below that of drunk driving, and no indication of any drugs in his system.

The scene on the bridge was brutally ugly and the personal devastation had a tremendous impact on the observations and conclusions of the many witnesses—a circumstance which later worked in the defendant's favor during trial.

I conducted an extensive investigation and carefully reviewed the discovery provided by the State. It was apparent that the witnesses' mob-like hate and anger against my client could possibly be turned to his benefit.

The accuracy of observation can be significantly impacted by the sight of mutilated human beings. The events on that summer night on the Mathis Bridge created a mob psychology. Everything the witnesses observed was tainted against J.G. Fortunately, for him, the police were intent on taking him into custody, an act which likely spared him from serious harm at the hands of the crowd on the bridge.

When people are upset and angry, they will release their emotions by willingly speaking to interested persons. The police and my investigator were such persons. Both accurately recorded the statements which turned out to significantly and materially vary in content. The same witness would alter the story for different listeners and all the stories differed from one another.

A car following J.G. before the accident had four occupants. One occupant reported J.G.'s vehicle was traveling at a high speed,

60 to 75 m.p.h., but not swerving. Another reported his vehicle was traveling at a normal speed, 30 to 40 m.p.h., but noticeably changing lanes and swerving. This problem plagued the prosecution.

The first trial took two weeks and was tried at the Toms River Court House, Judge William Huber presiding and Thomas Keleher, Esq. presenting the case for the State.

Judge Huber, a former county prosecutor and a mild-mannered individual, conducted this case as he had many others–fairly. He stayed out of the fray and gave an evenhanded charge. He kept his opinion as to the defendant's guilt out of his treatment of the case. The State was well represented by Mr. Keleher, a successful private attorney who served the State in a part-time capacity and afterwards became Chief Prosecutor and later, Mayor of Dover Township.

The State's case had serious problems with the inconsistency of the witnesses and their obvious effort to convict my client. A simple motion for sequestration (separation) of witnesses guaranteed a straight-forward test of accuracy. No witness was allowed to hear the testimony of the other witnesses.

The only thing all of the witnesses agreed on was that the accident was a horror. They could not agree on what or how it had occurred. The jury could not agree on a set of facts compelling a conviction. They deliberated for six days without reaching a verdict. Judge Huber declared a mistrial.

The Prosecutor's Office insisted on a retrial and the case was retried by the same judge and the same prosecutor. This time, the State decided to place the emphasis on some form of intoxicant, notwithstanding the lack of objective evidence to support the claim. It produced three "experts" who opined J.G. was under the influence of some drug and this caused the accident. The effort backfired. With the hostility of the witnesses, the jury saw the State's case as artificial, contrived and a vendetta. After a second two-week trial and two more days of jury deliberations, the jury acquitted J.G.

Judge Huber distinguished the bench by his totally impartial treatment of the matter. The factual weaknesses in the case, the police "experts" and mob-like psychology led to an acquittal because that should have been the result: There was a simple lack of persuasive evidence.

In the first trial, the varied witness testimony created confusion on the facts, leading to disagreement amongst the jury. In the second, the State's evident bias made it look contrived and led to reasonable doubt.

This case and the next are illustrative of how well the system operates when the judge remains impartial.

STATE v. S.

This vehicular homicide case arose out of a horrendous one-car accident occurring in Little Silver, Monmouth County, New Jersey. My client, a 19-year-old male, was accused of causing the death of two other youths thought to have been passengers in his vehicle.

Rumson Road is a winding, two-lane road beginning at the Rumson Bridge and winding through some of the finest and most expensive territory in New Jersey and probably the entire United States. One travels a path of old estates and modern/contemporary residential extravaganzas through Rumson and Fair Haven, concluding in Little Silver.

The speed limit varies between 25 and 40 miles per hour. This operator traveled this winding road at speeds between 75 and 110 m.p.h. At a straight run in Little Silver, he had roared around two slower-moving vehicles. When he pulled his vehicle back into the proper lane, he lost control.

The vehicle skidded on the shoulder, the rear end fishtailed, it rolled over two or three times, started to break up and then rolled into a large oak tree abutting Rumson Road. No product from Detroit was ever designed to take impacts such as those and retain its structural integrity or provide a secure haven for its occupants. The vehicle broke into four major and several minor pieces.

Likewise, the bodies of two of the occupants were broken into several pieces and scattered over several hundred feet of roadway, much like one might see at the site of an aircraft disaster.

The third occupant, my client, was miraculously thrown clear during the initial roll and had survived intact, though he sustained several broken bones and internal injuries.

Monmouth County residents may recall this case as the one where the First Aid Squads from Fair Haven and Little Silver publicly squabbled whether body bags should be standard issue for their ambulances. There had been some understandable unhappiness when First Aid members were forced to pick up body parts with no safe and private repository for them at the scene.

My client was removed to Riverview Hospital for medical treatment of his injuries. The police followed and attempted to obtain information and a statement from him. Fortunately, his injuries prevented him from speaking with them. In the interim, his parents contacted counsel who suggested he have an initial office consult with an attorney after release from hospitalization before giving any information to the police. He followed that advice and the police were compelled to conduct their investigation without his assistance, statements or information. His silence provided the only possible avoidance of criminal liability for this horrendous disaster.

The car was registered to S.'s father though prior to the occasion of the accident it had been driven by the two other occupants. If the car had been registered to my client, the State would have been able to secure an inference he had been driving the car. Without that inference, identification of the driver became a difficult problem.

The operators of the two slow-moving vehicles that the doomed vehicle had passed just prior to the accident had only seen the car for a few fleeting moments. They could only say the operator looked like a young person. An oncoming vehicle's occupants couldn't even say how many occupants there were in the other vehicle: That driver had wisely opted to pull off the roadway to avoid the oncoming rocket that became a death missile.

A Monmouth County Grand Jury had little difficulty in returning a two-count vehicular homicide indictment against my client, the sole surviving occupant of the death car. However, the standard to get an indictment is considerably more lenient than that of getting a conviction.

Assigned to prosecute was Michael Farren, an experienced and successful prosecutor who has since followed the path of public career by becoming a Superior Court judge. The trial judge was George Gray, a former Mayor of Red Bank, N.J., a former assistant prosecutor, and a former officer who had fought in the China and Southeast Asian theater of the Second World War. He had been appointed to the Monmouth County judiciary in the position of District Court judge and had spent his entire judicial career without promotion to a full County Court judgeship, let alone a Superior Court judge.

In the 1960s and 70s, the trial judge system was three-tiered for salary purposes, the lowest position being District Court judge. Even though the three positions required equal time and service and trial of the same matters, the political system retained these distinctions until the enlightened 80s when they all became Superior Court judges. The retention of this old, three-stratum system was somehow related to local control and the "good ol' boys club" of those days to receive the higher appointment and higher salary.

Eventually, the local politicians, who were supposed to put in the names for judicial appointments, stopped submitting the name of George Gray for elevation. So, Gray spent his entire career in the lowest-paying judicial office, victim of the crudest type of personal vindictiveness. Our twenty-first century judicial selection system has not improved much; we still suffer political problems with timely appointments and lack of quality appointments.

Unfortunately for Judge Gray, his physical faculties left him before those of his "enemy", and he languished at the bottom, forced to retire without ever attaining the complete dignity of the office all his brethren had secured. As a trial judge, George Gray could exhibit moments of legal brilliance, but also get hung up like a blundering idiot on some insignificant point. He is distinguished as being the only judge in New Jersey jurisprudence to grant a directed judgment of conviction in a criminal case. That action, reversed on appeal, demonstrated both his total lack of understanding of the nature of the criminal law process and how vulnerable he was to follow some thought to absurdity. Until George Gray, every lawyer and judge knew that in a contested jury criminal case, the jury decided guilt or innocence. That is the essence of our system.

During our trial, Judge Gray got hung up on a lost leader: how was the State going to prove the speed limit? This was the 'problem' that absorbed his energy and forced Prosecutor Farren into a blind alley. Nobody bothered to prove my client was the operator of the vehicle. The typical result-oriented judge would have bludgeoned his way into proving this key fact or sufficiently clouded the point, undercutting defense counsel's use of it in summation.

Because Judge Gray strayed from this key portion of the case, I was able to keep the jury's eye on the ball. Despite the horror of the case, they refused to be stampeded past proof of all of the elements. Nothing is more vital in defense of a criminal case than compelling the State to prove every element to secure a conviction. Where there is a paucity of proof, that is where counsel should expend their energies. Unfortunately, most trial judges take it upon themselves to ensure this doesn't occur. Because George Gray didn't see too well, this one got through and the defendant was acquitted. His guilt was not proven.

My client did not testify. The State could not call him to the stand, and my only obligation as defense counsel was to prevent him from testifying if I knew he was going to lie or make up facts. Once on the stand, of course, the State could examine him. I knew that if my client told the truth, it would provide evidence for the missing element of the State's case–the identity of the driver.

Some might feel the result was a miscarriage of justice. I do not. I fervently believe that tough cases test the system and here it was fully vindicated by the not-guilty verdict. Having the process work correctly is more important than the outcome of a single case.

These two case experiences are proof of the value of jury trials where trial judges do not interfere to get a result the court wants.

Vietnam and Its Impact on My Practice

W. V. Monmouth College (1969-1972)

I had a friend who was an economics professor at Monmouth College, West Long Branch, New Jersey. He was also a labor and political activist. Monmouth had been a two-year junior college which, shortly before his arrival, had become a full four-year private institution. The campus was steeped in the rich tradition of old Long Branch. It boasted the "Guggenheim Library" and the great "Wilson Hall," two landmarks from the heyday of the Long Branch of the early 20th Century.

When W. arrived, the Vietnam War had become a highly charged political issue and the Monmouth campus was a hot bed of student activism. A labor union "FAMCO", the Faculty Administration of Monmouth College (now University), had recently been formed and there was considerable agitation for improving the lot of the professional staff. As a young professor who related well with the students and the relatively young staff, W. became a spokesperson and leader. The administration of the College was slightly to the right of conservative Barry Goldwater and had absolutely no use for the double threat posed by this young and articulate professor.

So, the order went out to his Department Chairman, Professor R. T.: Get rid of this non-tenured individual.

Professor R.T., a colorless and obscure man, recommended that Monmouth not renew W.'s contract for the following year. As a relatively new employee, W. did not enjoy the protections of tenure and therefore could be non-renewed without cause. By that time, however, FAMCO had managed to secure some minimum procedural due process rights for its personnel. After paying lip-service to that procedure, Monmouth told W. he was through.

Since the school was a private institution, it need not afford the due process rights constitutionally required of a public employer. After reviewing the situation, I concluded his only remedy was a claim under the National Labor Relations Act (NLRA). His discharge had in part been motivated by his labor activity in deviation of standards of academic freedom and in violation of the National Labor Act. That law forbids employers from terminating employee because of pro-union activity or for agitating for better working conditions.

We decided to go ahead with an unfair labor charge against Monmouth College. Administration of the NLRA was delegated to the National Labor Relations Board, which had regional field offices. Our claim was within the jurisdiction of the Newark Regional office. Following standard procedure, that office conducted its investigation and, after reviewing the facts and circumstances, found sufficient evidence to issue a formal charge. The procedure then required an administrative law judge, who rode the circuit in the various NLRB regions, be brought in to try the case and make a recommendation to the NLRB in Washington, D. C.

Into Newark rode the single rudest official I have ever run across. Accustomed to hearing disputes between arrogant management types and ill-educated union bosses, the field of academia was totally foreign to him. Fortunately for us, Monmouth College had an experienced and well-polished labor counsel. The nature of opposing counsel can make a trial miserable or pleasurable. The one saving grace in this matter was having John Yauch and Frank Peterpaul as my adversaries.

Judge Sahm, pronounced like the 23rd of the Old Testament, didn't initially understand either our claim or the college's defense. After two and a half days of a sometimes-acrimonious hearing, he reserved decision. We were resigned to a dismissal. After nearly two months of waiting, I received a true surprise when we received his opinion.

This well-traveled veteran had concluded Professor R.T. had been untruthful in claiming W was fired -because of departmental need and not his protected pro-union or job condition activities. To Judge Sahm it had simply been a gut call that the "needs" of the department meant the "need" to be free of a union/student activist like my client. Sahm ordered him reinstated with back pay and directed the College to post notice of its improper conduct.

Naturally the College wouldn't accept the order and appealed to the National Labor Relations Board. I had been told the Board reversed its administrative judges about ten percent of the time. On questions of credibility, the chances of reversal were even slimmer. Wrong again!

The Board was unhappy with Sahm's reasoning and findings and sent the case back for rehearing on some obscure issue. When we reconvened for the new hearing, not only was Sahm rude with both counsel, but he challenged the Board, digging in his heels and sticking to his initial position. Refusing to address the Board's request for supplemental findings, Sahm once again ruled W. had been terminated in part for his union activities and directed reinstatement. Though we were getting the result we thought was deserved, my client was stuck in a power play between the Board and this strong judge.

This time, on the re-appeal back to the Board, I wasn't very confident. I knew the Board, loaded with Nixon appointees, was conservative and would not be enthralled with W.'s anti-war and FAMCO activities. It was one thing to condone pro-labor tactics by an assembly-line union; quite another to tolerate radicalism on a college campus where the minds of our youth were being shaped. This time I was right, and we washed out.

The Board had no use for this type of claim. It struck too deeply at their basic conservative traditions. This was a time of real fear of campus radicalism. They were prepared to give justice to the–union or the worker in the factory where the issues were money and the interests truly private. However, when it came to the minds of our young, this Board wanted only peace and quiet for our college campuses. They concluded the best needs of the economics department and the school was for W. to depart.

The young professor was crestfallen by this turn of events. He now knew why he had been dismissed. The idealism he shared with other FAMCO members and students was shattered. Those in control of government and the judiciary have their own ideals: a quiet study hall. They would accept a little debate and criticism, but when the debate turned real and the questions hard and posed by intelligent and strong persons, the lid came down. I took an appeal from the NLRB decision to the Third Circuit Court of Appeals in Philadelphia, my adversary moving my admission before that court.

Shortly, after oral argument, we received a one-line opinion stating there was no basis to disturb the NLRB decision. The battle was over, we'd run out of ammunition and W. was banished from Monmouth College forever. He'd discovered that the philosophical link between college administration, NLRB and the court system was solid.

Those in power and control wanted order and to be left alone. Perhaps it has always been that way.

I was disappointed in the result, but content in two ways: (1) I had the satisfaction of knowing we had actually proven our case before a two-fisted guy whose gut told him we were right; and (2) the case confirmed my thesis the system would react to certain challenges in a certain fashion.

The case reminded me of why golf "hackers" continue to toil at their game. You can hit fifteen terrible shots in a row but then drive one like a pro. That limited success is enough satisfaction to keep you going. In this case, as in others, there had been enough success to keep me going.

In human terms, though, the net result was the derailment of a promising teaching career, a truly real loss from legal nonsense. A talented, energetic idealistic professor lost his career and probably a bit of his idealism. One must work hard to retain idealism, at times a very challenging task.

Conscientious Objectors
(1967-1975)

Vietnam brought an explosion of anti-war agitation. One legal field experiencing this explosion was in claims for conscientious objector status. Those claims arose both in-service and in avoiding entry into the military. In the extreme, they involved defense of a federal criminal prosecution for draft evasion or unauthorized absences (AWOL).

Many decisions eventually clarified how far the establishment would go in tolerating this type of thinking. What emerged was a very subjective standard: did the Department of Defense (D.O.D.) have a basis in fact for denying the claim of entitlement to conscientious objector (CO) status? The claim of being a conscientious objector itself was a concept emanating from an Act of Congress, not from any constitutional precept.

D.M. v. DEPARTMENT OF ARMY

My first case in this area was of Lt. D. M., a regular Army officer who came to me after receiving notice from the Department of Defense he did not qualify for in-service C.O. status. The Government required an applicant demonstrate an objection to all military conflict, not just one or some. That objection had to be based on a religious or significant ethical belief. The Department of Defense felt D.M.'s objection was not to all war, just the Vietnam conflict.

After reviewing the matter, I determined the proper remedy was to file a Petition for Writ of Habeas Corpus with the U.S. Federal District Court in Newark. The purpose of such a petition is to obtain an order from the court requiring whoever was holding that person to deliver him or her to the court for freedom. This was a civil remedy embossed on our Constitution to protect our citizens from improper deprivation of freedom. Historically it is sometimes called the "Great Writ."

When his case came up for hearing in the Federal court in Newark, several high-ranking military personnel appeared, in addition to several newspersons.

Judge James Coolahan concluded the D.O.D. did not have a basis in fact to deny C.O. status to my client. In doing so he set forth clear criteria to be followed by Department of Defense officials. Judge Coolahan's decision was not appealed to the Court of Appeals, and D.M. was honorably discharged and returned to civilian status as a result of his deeply and honestly held conviction against war.

With this decision as well as several other such rulings, the D.O.D. began to consider the numerous applications in a different light, resulting in an increase of D.O. D.-awarded CO status. The courts also clarified when claims of CO status could be used in defense of criminal cases brought in draft related matters.

I note these rulings and the D.O.D.'s acquiescence as an odd but pleasantly surprising reaction by the military establishment to rulings such as in D.M.'s case. The military, a bastion of discipline, overcame its institutional bias against C.O. applications in a positive way. This point is emphasized in stark contrast to the unremitting institutional bias in many of the other cases to be discussed. Judges and our civilian politicians do not change their thinking as does a discipline-based bureaucracy like our armed forces.

The awe and respect for discipline ingrained in the military mind made it possible for them to put aside their natural antipathy for C.O. claims. Its respect for order imposed on it by its own institution, made it respect the orders imposed on it by court authorities. The D.O.D. stepped up and in line and began to honestly administer its own CO regulations.

The courts remained reluctant to construe the law broadly to aid many anti-war persons, while the Department of Defense can be complimented for its subsequent treatment of C.O. applicants. Very ironic!

The contrast was best illustrated during a trial of a person accused of draft evasion when he refused induction into the U.S. Army. This was a federal criminal trial at the famous "Foley Square Court House" in lower Manhattan. Presiding at the trial was the well-known federal figure, Judge Charles Stewart.

THE DRAFT "DODGER"

The U.S. Attorney was a great big imposing man with the reputation of never losing a draft-evader case. This was my first and last trial in Foley Square. It took place over six trial days during the late 1960's and I've forgotten the name of my client, but I will never forget the events.

It is hard to express my feelings. The trial of this matter in the hallmark of the federal establishment left me in awe. It was a challenge just to get on the train each day for the commute to that imposing hall of justice.

The judge and prosecutor made no bones about it: Get the case over with and get this disloyal individual into Federal Prison for two or three years, where he belonged. But the worse they became, the more I "dug in my heels." Because the government had been having its own way with Judge Stewart for some time, they were out of shape, and a little sloppy for a full-scale battle.

During the course of the trial, the U.S. Attorney had forgotten to call a representative of the draft board as a witness to prove the defendant had not appeared to take his oath on the appointed day. My summation to the jury came first, and I pointed out how the government had failed to prove this essential element of the charge. This argument cut deeply into the veracity of all their charges, much like their failure to prove the driver's identity in State v. S.

I opted not to call the defendant to the stand because if he testified, he would have to admit he had failed to appear. Under the law, if a defendant chooses not to testify, neither the prosecutor nor the court can comment on that failure as an admission of guilt.

The U.S. Attorney, in his summation, sought to make up for this paucity of proof. He said to the jury, "Look at the defendant; does he have a uniform on? Would we have brought this case if he had showed up?"

I went crazy! That was an improper comment calling for immediate intervention by the court. I objected. The court excused the jury. The Prosecutor tried to be physically intimidating, his body language letting me know he'd love to toss me out of the 25th floor window of the courtroom. I asked for a mistrial with prejudice.

Though he knew I was legally correct, Judge Stewart coldly rejected my claim. Instead, he overruled the objection, told the U.S. Attorney to get to another point, and allowed the case to go to the jury.

He avoided a clash with the Government to let the jury do his dirty work. However, that jury would not be used. Instead, after five days of fighting and arguing, they reported they were hopelessly deadlocked and were discharged.

This small victory broke the U.S. Attorney's winning streak, itself another illustration of judicial failure. Compare their response with that of the military regarding Conscientious

Objectors. Our courts could not carry out their constitutional mandate, while our military could and did. It was not until the U.S. Supreme Court decision in Clay v. U.S., 403 U.S. 698 (1971), that the courts finally yielded at all. Thousands of young men lost freedom and other precious rights as a result of civilian courts' political stubbornness.

Labor Cases

During the early years, I began representing public employee groups in their issues with their public employers. This included recognition issues, disciplinary matters and job continuation cases, as well as criminal and labor strife cases. I have divided this section into two employment types; teacher matters and police representation.

TEACHER MATTERS

I became the attorney for several local teacher associations in Monmouth County. These included Asbury Park Education Association, Neptune Teachers Association, Long Branch Education Association, Freehold Regional Education Association and the Manalapan Teachers Association.

This work included labor negotiations, handling non-tenure dismissals, suits over alleged discrimination and the most difficult cases involving labor stoppages which, invariably ended up in Chancery Division of the Superior Court.

This experience brought me into contact with very interesting and well-spoken individuals as well as some rather bizarre ones, very different than the people on the Board of Education side of the ledger. Almost without exception, Board members were stuffy, highly conservative people who were extremely difficult to compromise with, and who could, at times, be arbitrary and beyond reason. The labor people were a breath of fresh air. The members of the judiciary thrown into that mix tried at times to be fair, but mostly acted as an annex to the Board of Education.

In many respects, the NJEA, the statewide organization for teachers, had created a great deal of hostility within the state toward the teachers' movement. It had organized the state through field offices with its employees acting as advisors to and for the local organizations.

The NJEA also operated a legal aid program, approving certain attorneys to represent teachers and locals in various legal endeavors. I and my firm were approved in that regard.

Some of this work produced published opinions all the way from the Commissioner of Education through the New Jersey Supreme Court.

Long Branch Education Association v. Long Branch Board of Education 150 N.J. Super 262 (App. Div., 1976) Aff'd 73 N.J.-461 (1977). Board allowed to increase teacher duties and length of workday without agreement or compensation.

Red Bank Teachers Association v. ARC and Red Bank Board of Education (6-8-81) and Manalapan Education Association v. Manalapan Board of Education cases (12-13-78) and (1-30-81) 187 N.J. Super 426 (App. Div., 1981). Reversals for procedural violations by the Board of Education.

What these cases demonstrate is that courts would provide some degree of fairness when it came to procedure, but on matters of substance they were 100% on the side of the public employer. If it came to drawing a favorable inference on behalf of labor, we were out of luck.

In many non-renewals of non-tenured teachers, the office of the Commissioner and the deputies who adjudicated these cases simply refused any and all reasonable inference to set aside a local board's whitewash of a superintendent's vendetta against the teacher. After the first few years, the NJEA finally stopped underwriting those cases.

On labor actions like strikes, which are illegal by public employees, the courts would not delve into the irrational, stubborn and arbitrary actions by the Board and its agents which had driven law-abiding citizens to break the law. The court would break the strike, leaving the local teachers to accept "table scraps" and face severe penalties.

While it was clear that strikes by public employees were against the law and policy, public entities like Boards of Education were under an affirmative duty to negotiate in good faith. The courts vigorously enforced the no-strike policy but would not get involved in enforcing the good faith portion of the process.

My work was to try and keep the damage to a minimum and hold my temper as I sat negotiating with the Board's hired guns. These were usually lawyers who enjoyed dragging out the process and billing the Board for their own bad faith intransigence.

Ironically, I was terminated from the NJEA list of attorneys in the 80s because I'd represented Judge Thomas L. Yaccarino in his disciplinary case, which was brought by the Supreme Court. He had jailed Freehold teachers for a strike in the 60s. The NJEA never forgot that and took it out on me because I dared to represent he, who to them, was a pariah.

POLICE MATTERS

While involved with teacher labor work, I also actively represented the police unions (PBA's) in the Borough of Highlands and Borough of Tinton Falls. I also represented a few officers in some bizarre situations.

I educated members of the police force on public employee rights to collective negotiation of contracts with the public employer, then negotiated those contracts, which became the model for years to come.

There were two cases combining my police work and criminal law which demonstrate how the power structure operated when it came to police misconduct.

State v. R.S.

Uncle Henry's Auction, located in Neptune Township, New Jersey was a predecessor of "Best Buy" and "P.C. Richards." One night my client "S.", a Neptune Township police officer, responded to an alarm of a break-in· at that store. Upon arrival, "S." found his fellow officers in the middle of removing TV sets and related appliances. How should he respond to his compatriots breaking the law in his presence?

He stopped them from continuing, walked away without making any arrests and filed a police report that failed to accurately describe what had occurred. However, another member of the force reported the incident to the command. After an investigation, my client was brought up on departmental charges and faced an indictment for official misconduct.

The departmental charges were heard before the Neptune Township governing body on a night in July 1970 during the race riots in Asbury Park and Neptune Township. Just to get to that hearing, which the Township Committee refused to adjourn, I had to drive through roadblocks manned by State Troopers and National Guard troops. What an experience.

After a rather brief hearing and an even briefer deliberation, the Township Committee announced it had discharged my client. No real consideration was given to the extreme situation with which he had been confronted. While his account of the incident had been incomplete, he had cooperated with the internal investigation and stopped the crime in-progress. No matter, he was disgracefully terminated by his employer. Once more we saw how the public body lacked any insight or public fairness. Naturally, on appeal the Superior Court upheld the bidding of the local power body. No consideration was given to the extreme conflict and psychological anguish my client was subjected to. I cannot envision a veteran officer doing anything different.

Adding insult to injury, the Monmouth County Grand Jury indicted my client for official misconduct. After the trial, the jury showed more insight and sensibility than the Township Committee and acquitted my client, again illustrating how juries instinctively do the right thing when not tainted by overreaching trial judges.

This characterized many of my experiences during the early years. When allowed the complete story, the jury would do the right thing. Here, it would not criminalize a simple omission from a police report. On the other hand, the judges, government and bureaucracy had a hard time with the right thing.

My client had been confronted with an extreme emotional challenge. Men who he worked with had been caught breaking the law. He had stopped them before they completed their crime. Yet, he wouldn't formally charge them or complete a report which clearly stated what they were doing. The employing local government couldn't acknowledge this without discharging him from his office. Yet, a jury had the compassion to acquit him of criminal activity.

Which action would you have taken?

Any recitation of this period of my practice would be incomplete without noting the infamous Long Branch Police Department juvenile sexual misconduct case.

State v. R.G.

In 1974, several uniformed Long Branch police officers were arrested for sexual misconduct with a 16-year-old female at the West End Fire House.

The next day I was retained by officer "R.G.", who related a story which seemed to come from a racy novel. While on duty in uniform he received a call from a fellow officer telling him to show up at the West End Fire House to get a "treat." Off he went to an encounter which would permanently alter his life.

Upon arrival he was taken upstairs and ushered into a small room. In it was a young woman completely naked who offered him her body to do with whatever he wished. My client fondled her and had her perform fellatio on him. After climax, he simply left the premises and returned to his patrol duty.

His actions and those of another fifteen officers would not remain hidden for very long.

After an internal investigation, assisted by the West Long Branch Police Department and the Monmouth County Prosecutor's Office, indictments were returned against many of Long Branch's "finest". The scandal was immense and drove one of the officers to commit suicide.

Notwithstanding the gravity of this mass crime, the entire group was permitted to resign and receive suspended sentences for official misconduct. The young woman, the daughter of a local minister, became pregnant. We never found out what happened to her afterwards. Several prominent Long Branch businessmen were also implemented, but never charged.

Had these events occurred in the 21st century, all of the officers would have been required to register as "sex offenders" and likely received prison sentences of seven years or more, though generally, society still protects its police officers.

The idea that fifteen regular police officers had a sexual encounter with a child, were permitted to escape incarceration and any serious consequences other than resignation is shocking, to say the least. The court system was directly involved in this miscarriage as was the County Prosecutor.

What truths have I learned?

- Judges have tremendous power and if they use it in an overarching fashion, justice is denied. If not misled, our juries will do the right thing and follow the evidence;
- The establishment is sterile, lacks fairness and expects judges to fall in line. Many will;
- Justice is hard to come by but can be achieved with insight, great effort, great patience and some good luck.

What I learned from these first fifteen years of practice, was that, in law, the people defending it, interpreting it and trying to change it was much of what my education at Rutgers and my father had taught me to expect. That would change during the next twenty years.

The Middle Years: 1980–2000

In 1981, I became involved in a matter that shook my belief in our judicial system almost to the point of complete cynicism: representation of a Superior Court judge in a removal and attorney discipline matter. I say 'almost' only because I still occasionally see opinions written in the highest and best tradition of our common law.

These include several New Jersey Supreme Court opinions demonstrating our top court can show true enlightenment and accept varying notions of what is fair and just. Sometimes, the Appellate Division and trial court decisions share that same insight.

Sadly, it's been my experience that many times, they do not.

The Case of Thomas L. Yaccarino

Maybe someday a respected, deliberative body will convene to look back and unemotionally analyze what happened to one of New Jersey's premier jurists, Thomas L. Yaccarino. Yaccarino came through the system as a trial prosecutor, an astute appellate advocate, a tough trial judge and ultimately, a Chancellor in the Equity Part of the N.J. Superior Court.

As a result of an incident commencing in the spring of 1981 and several subsequent events, a proud and distinguished leader of the bench perished, after first being reduced to near rubble. Perceived as an angel fallen from grace, he became a threat to one of the imperial guards, i.e. the Chief Justice; one that had to be dealt with in an extreme sense.

The decade of the 80s in New Jersey jurisprudence could be aptly termed the Yaccarino Decade. For more than eight years the battle raged until finally, in late 1989, the last legalistic act concluded in this tragedy for the man and his beloved system. The battle was over, on May 11, 1993 when he finally succumbed, his heart broken. Shortly thereafter, his primary antagonist, Chief Justice Robert Wilentz, also died.

I served as Judge Yaccarino's lead counsel among many distinguished attorneys, including a former judge and a man who would become Attorney General of New Jersey. Ultimately, I remained his only legal support. My worst fears regarding our judicial system were realized in its politics and serious flaws.

The recruitment and training camps for our judges is usually some form of public legal position. The most public and vocal is service as public prosecutor. Early in his legal career, Tom Yaccarino served as Assistant Prosecutor for Monmouth County. He gained an admirable reputation as an articulate and proficient trial advocate and subsequently as a well-spoken appellate advocate. During his prosecutorial service, Monmouth County had a series of high-visibility cases including some very famous murder trials, as well as a celebrated rape case. In all these matters, Yaccarino's presence on the prosecutor's team was keenly felt. Having grown up at the Jersey Shore, Asbury/Neptune area, he knew many people and was very active and influential within the public sector, particularly in the training of police personnel.

Ironically, Yaccarino was appointed to the bench illegally. In New Jersey, a judge must have been admitted to the bar for at least ten years before being eligible for appointment to the trial bench. Yaccarino hadn't served the requisite period of time when appointed. That question was raised on an appeal from a criminal conviction by a defendant who alleged this defect vitiated his judgment of conviction. The Appellate Division, however, created a new category, "de facto judge", to escape the constitutional ten-year mandate. The resourcefulness of our judiciary in avoiding legal pitfalls was thus employed on Yaccarino's way in as well as, later, on his way out.

During his tenure on the bench, he became a living legend. In the criminal law field, he had a reputation as a very tough and result-oriented jurist. Many defense counsels regretted vigorous advocacy in his courtroom. However, his strong suit was his sentencing philosophy being, perhaps, the most enlightened sentencing judge in our courts. When explaining a sentence, he sold listeners on his rationale and built acceptance of the disposition, even by the defendant recipients. If a criminal defendant had a chance for rehabilitation, Yaccarino gave it to him. His was the era in which a judge would use the sentencing process to get the defendant's attention.

Every especially difficult or complicated matter was shipped off to his courtroom. He was, perhaps, too sure of himself and always confident his was the correct solution. Here was a jurist who became the law itself: this transformation would become his undoing. By feeding him the especially difficult cases, the system fed an insatiable personality. The more cases sent his way, the bigger the balloon lifting him above the rest of us mortals. By the spring of 1981, that balloon was ready to burst. His descent into personality dysfunction and poor judgment was hastened by open-heart surgery.

While at home one evening late in the spring of 1981, the judge read a publication from the community college where one of his daughters matriculated. A front-page story detailed how his daughter and her little dog had tangled with a campus policeman, been arrested, man-handled and in his mind, thoroughly humiliated. The events sent Yaccarino on a wild sled ride down a steep hill, out of control, setting in motion a series of events that led to his removal from the bench, loss of his license to practice law, and ultimately his very life.

Hearing of the possible mistreatment of his daughter, Yaccarino was determined to force a review of the arresting officer's actions. He sought to bring upon that individual an investigation of the incident and encouraged the filing of cross-complaints against him. He also called the Chief of Campus Police and demanded some investigation looking towards the initiation of disciplinary action. Imagine the nerve of this father/judge. He tried to see to it that the police officer who allegedly assaulted his daughter would be subjected to some official review of his conduct. For that attempt, several canons of judicial conduct were violated and, therefore, formal proceedings before several august personages looked into his "aberrant" behavior.

Testimony at the judge's disciplinary hearings revealed the officer, a large fellow over two-hundred pounds and standing above six feet tall, had been forced to arrest the judge's four-foot, ten-inch, ninety-five-pound daughter and her dog, which weighed in at less than 5 pounds. During this action, this professional put his hands all over the chest of the culprit and after a highly physical arrest and handcuffing, had her processed at the station house and ultimately released.

The progeny of the problem which led to this police action was Ms. Yaccarino's failure to have her dog on a leash at the college bookstore. The animal had been sitting quietly before the encounter when this official action–and the resulting fray–occurred.

Ironically, there never was a formal hearing into the conduct of that arresting officer. It was a laugh for him and a disaster for this caring father.

The conduct of sitting judges is monitored by an agency known as the Advisory Committee on Judicial Conduct (A.C.J.C). That agency became aware of the charges against Yaccarino's daughter in the municipal court and sent a representative to sit in on the proceedings to determine if parent Yaccarino was present for the public hearing. At the time the A.C.J.C. was chaired by a former Supreme Court Justice who personally disliked the judge and had previously castigated him in front of other judges.

Yaccarino saw the A.C.J.C. as a threat to the independence of individual judges. The Chairman saw the Committee in a much more benevolent fashion. Prior to filing formal complaints against Yaccarino, there had been a series of written exchanges between the Chairman, his secretary and Yaccarino. The letters reflected their clash of views.

The Committee issued formal charges against Yaccarino, including charges he had not properly comported himself while on the bench[5], and allegations of improper behavior related to the daughter/dog incident.

I was initially retained as his attorney to defend all the charges. Shortly after, I was asked to share the defense responsibilities with another lawyer who was a little more mainstream than me. Joseph Dempsey, a brilliant man, joined the defense team. We split responsibilities with Joe handling the judicial deportment cases and I the "dog" case.

Seeing the case as a long, arduous one, Joe wanted to raise money for a defense fund. To do this he brought in one Theodore Geiser. Geiser was a member of a distinguished firm in Newark with connections at the highest places in state and national government. Though ostensibly there to help us raise funds, I believe he was also brought in to broaden the respectability of the defense. Ironically, his addition to the team guaranteed the end of Yaccarino's judgeship.

For unbeknownst to us, Yaccarino had been talking with a litigant about purchasing a house in Sea Girt, New Jersey, from an estate involved in post-judgment arbitration before the Chancery Division of Superior Court.

The case, involving something in excess of $15 million, had been settled and Yaccarino was presiding over the case not so much as judge but as an arbitrator. The litigant was setting the judge up, dangling the property in front of his nose at a ridiculously low price and taping some or all of their conversations. He wanted to use the taped conversations to force the judge to do his bidding or get the settlement set aside or secure a jurist friendlier to his side of the matter. This was blackmail, yet

---

[5] Yaccarino as a trial judge could be rude, sarcastic, and bombastic. Several litigants, including some attorneys, had complained of his bench conduct.

after it came to light it was ignored by the prosecutors and justices alike.

Though Yaccarino was being suckered along by the bait of getting a beautiful home in a respectable area for a very modest sum, no contract was ever signed, no money passed hands and no friendly decision was ever rendered. The judge toyed with the idea for a few months. While he talked about it, he was being taped. Even before the existence and content of the tapes became public, he'd already decided there'd be no transaction and the litigant had been so advised.

Disgruntled, the litigant shared the tapes with a well-placed county Democratic leader to force Yaccarino off his case. That person, no stranger to controversy, shared the tapes with his long-time friend and attorney Richard Bonello, brother John Bonello and the local Democratic leaders. Seeing the situation ripe for exploitation, the Bonello brothers reached out to their attorney, coincidentally one Ted Geiser. Geiser went to Yaccarino with rather jaded advice. If followed, Yaccarino would be removed from the case, the litigant would achieve his goal, and Geiser and the Bonellos would achieve theirs—a new public attorney position and just maybe that fine piece of real estate in Sea Girt on the cheap.

Geiser suggested Yaccarino claim illness, sign himself into a hospital and put in a claim for retirement disability. The tapes would then be history. If Yaccarino didn't have the 'right' doctor, Geiser had some recommendations. Neither Geiser nor the Bonellos knew Yaccarino was already suffering very significant physical debilities which did actually justify his subsequent disability pension. Nor did they consider the fact that he was already on the ACJC's radar for the "dog" case and the bad deportment claims.

The judge knew he was being manipulated in some dark plot. With his personality, he wasn't about to take Geiser's advice or, for that matter, any sound legal advice at all.

Geiser and Yaccarino reached out for the other attorneys in his case. A fateful meeting between counsel was held at my office on a Saturday afternoon. We heard the tapes and discussed not only their significance but also our professional responsibilities and whether we should secure counsel on that question.

Over my objection, Yaccarino was requested to come to the meeting. I left, replaced by John Bonello. In my absence, Yaccarino and his other attorneys and advisors argued for hours in a stormy session. Geiser resigned as Yaccarino's attorney when he wouldn't take his advice but continued to participate in the discussions. Yaccarino accused John Bonello of conspiring with his brother and the Democratic leader to secure a personal gain. The situation became ever more bitter and divisive and finally broke up without resolution.

The following day, a Sunday, I received a call from Joe Dempsey saying he wanted out of the case because he had been told Yaccarino had told Richard Bonello to have the litigant destroy the tapes or to make up a false affidavit on their disposition.

Geiser was in a direct conflict of interest, being attorney for both Yaccarino and the Bonellos. That violation never concerned the purists who later reviewed Yaccarino's conduct.

I set up a meeting with Yaccarino that same evening to try to give some direction to the unfolding disaster. In the interim, Geiser told me he had decided to call a highly placed judicial ethics official and turn Yaccarino in. The Geiser side sensed they would at best look bad, and at worst be in trouble if Yaccarino himself contacted the Supreme Court to reveal the tapes and the overall situation.

At our meeting that Sunday evening, we decided Judge Yaccarino would call the Chief Justice on Monday and explain the situation to him.

Instead, that Monday morning I received a call from the Assignment Judge of Monmouth County who asked me whether I knew anything about any tapes. On Sunday, Mr. Geiser had contacted certain officials and the word had spread like wildfire through officialdom. Both a criminal and judicial investigation into Yaccarino's conduct had been initiated immediately.

That following week I asked to meet with the Acting Chief Justice, who first agreed to, then canceled, our meeting. Instead, Yaccarino was asked to take a medical leave, which he did. Shortly thereafter, the Newark Star Ledger ran a front-page story with both the Chief Justice and Attorney General confirming a criminal and ethics investigation into the matter.

After a two-month investigation with immunity granted to several of the witnesses, the Attorney General announced no criminal charges would be instituted against Yaccarino out of the Sea Girt, N.J. tape matter.

Consequently, Yaccarino and I were summoned to the chambers of the Chief Justice in Perth Amboy, New Jersey. There I was treated to one of the most astounding scenes of my entire legal career.

The Chief Justice's chambers were located at the top of a bank building in Perth Amboy, a moderately-sized city located north of the Raritan River in the heart of industrial New Jersey. The city had seen better days and was suffering problems similar to those of other inner cities in the state. The chambers had been redone and were a breath of fresh air perched high above the deteriorating surroundings. We were ushered into Robert Wilentz's private office and seated in front of his desk.

The Chief Justice was blessed with dark, curly hair, was young-looking, and spoke with great dignity in a melodious voice. He expressed his delight Yaccarino was feeling better and noted he'd received a letter from the judge's personal physician attesting to his improved state of health.

After exchanging further pleasantries, Wilentz said he was ready to put Yaccarino back to work in the Superior Court. The court is divided into a Law Division, which convenes primarily for jury trials, and a Chancery Division, Yaccarino's trial bench empire. The Chief Justice suggested Yaccarino move to the Law Division while the judicial investigation was continuing.

With that, Yaccarino slammed his raincoat, which had been sitting across his lap, onto the floor. He demanded to know why he was being reduced in responsibility and punished without any hearing or a finding of misconduct. While the Chief Justice politely tried to explain, Yaccarino was rude and interrupted him, complaining the negative publicity had been generated by the Chief Justice's own improper statements confirming the investigations. I looked for a safe exit. There was none. The conversation ended with the Chief Justice directing Yaccarino to return to the Law Division if he wanted to work, and that was final.

When that confrontation concluded, it was apparent to me, that the Chief Justice had decided my client could not remain a judge. Such a rude man could not be trusted to participate in the sensitive and eggshell-type New Jersey judicial system. He would not accept orders as a good team man should. He could not acknowledge authority over him and was unreasonable and unyielding.

As we left the chambers, I felt that what had begun as a chance at salvation had turned into a disaster. The future held only trouble for my judge client. He'd turned an encounter with his boss who was welcoming him back to work, into an ugly scene. Proof was delivered firsthand to the Chief Justice that this man could no longer be one of the brethren of the New Jersey bench.

After Yaccarino returned to work, the slow process of moving the pending charges before the A.C.J.C. continued to unfold. The "Sea Girt house affair" charges were also pushed to the same Committee.

Meanwhile, the office of the New Jersey Attorney General initiated an investigation into the nature of Yaccarino's interest in two liquor license establishments. Judges were not supposed to have economic interests, other than investments, beyond their judicial functions. In typical heavy-handed fashion, Alcoholic Beverage Control troopers made unannounced seizures at one of the bars. This seize-now-but-discuss-later approach is standard practice in the heavily regulated liquor industry. Yaccarino's interests in those two ventures joined the other charges in sinking his judgeship.

Concerned with a possible conflict, should any lawsuits arise concerning the two establishments, Yaccarino had not permitted his name to appear on the liquor license application, even though he and his wife partially owned the land where the establishments were located. Only his wife's name appeared on the licenses. On seizure of records, the A.B.C. charged the licensees under an arcane law of 'undisclosed ownership'. That law prevented disqualified persons or those of unacceptable character secretly owning liquor licenses.

Aimed at those with criminal records or other undesirables, they read it to apply to the judge and he was called on the judicial carpet for this "errant" behavior. Further, the Attorney General contended Yaccarino's active participation in that investment violated the law proscribing gainful economic activity by sitting judges. No regulations or meaningful guidelines had ever been issued under that law, nor were there any prior precedents. Those charges proceeded against him on an ad hoc basis.

Meanwhile, the first set of charges, the dog case and the judicial deportment matter, were called for hearing before the A.C.J.C. The hearings commenced in the old Supreme Court conference room in Trenton. The Committee was chaired by the old enemy of Yaccarino. Purportedly to assure fairness and balance to the proceedings other members included a former attorney general, a newspaper publisher, and a writer. Too bad the proceedings weren't videotaped; talk about the old "We'll give him a fair trial then hang him" adage. This one was a classic. At one point, the Chairman insisted on calling Yaccarino as a witness.

The court rule under which the proceedings were governed, left that decision up to the judge if he wished to testify at those hearings, in recognition that a sitting judge was a part of the sovereign and not just another defendant. Notwithstanding the clear meaning of the rule, the Chairman insisted on provoking a confrontation and directed Yaccarino to testify.

In order to avoid a contempt charge or worse, I immediately applied to a Justice of the Supreme Court to reverse the directive to testify. After some argument at the Justice's chambers, the Justice basically blinked and said, "Fellows, just work it out. I don't wanna get involved."

This was the law in operation at its finest hour. Nobody wanted to do anything disagreeable to a fellow lodge member, and we were forced to go back and play by the Chairman's arbitrary and illegal rules. The witnesses paraded in and out and our hearings concluded. The outcome was never in doubt.

Yaccarino, a staunch ally of the palace guard, always believed his friends in high places would never let him down. I just as firmly believed those 'friends' could not be relied on. We even discussed the matter in those terms.

The ink was hardly dry on the Committee report which roundly condemned him for his conduct, when hearings in the taping case started before the same A.C.J.C. Fortunately for me, - because I and members of my firm were witnesses, I didn't have responsibility on that hearing.

For a portion of that case, we had retained the services of former U.S. Attorney for New Jersey, Robert Del Tufo. He was a distinguished member of the bar and had demonstrated his mettle years before by speaking out against the government's prosecution of former Senator Harrison Williams. He even went on and served as Attorney General of New Jersey. I bet his C.V. did not include participation as counsel for Thomas L. Yaccarino.

In some ways, the Yaccarino matter paralleled the Williams matter. In both, the method of prosecution and institutional evil may have been more pernicious and pervasive than the individual wrongs that had been committed. The Williams story was recounted in the movie "American Hustle." Yaccarino's story showed a side of the legal system equally dark. It might make an even better movie.

The Sea Girt house case defense had two primary elements. First, much of the evidence came through attorney/client privilege violations. Second, Yaccarino was the victim of a conspiracy. The Committee, bent on Yaccarino's removal, showed little interest in either defense. In one stormy session, Del Tufo actually heard ethnic slurs made against Yaccarino by a committee member.

Shortly before the Committee finished its work, the defense team succeeded in convincing Yaccarino to submit an application for a disability retirement based on his serious and ongoing health problems. Under New Jersey law, a sitting judge may retire at 75 per cent of salary if his health prevents him from fulfilling his duties as a judge. Yaccarino's health problems had complicated and probably exacerbated his irascible personality.

After Yaccarino's filing, the Chief Justice called for an independent medical examination which confirmed the "claim. However, the court did not immediately act on the application, holding it until February 1984 for fear it might lose jurisdiction to remove him if it acted favorably on his application for disability. It did not want to "moot out" its disciplinary action against him by approving his disability retirement.

Meanwhile, the A.C.J.C. report regarding the 'house/tape' case was released to the court and the parties. There were no surprises. In all, the A.C.J.C. recommended filing formal removal proceedings against Judge Yaccarino. On February 1, 1984 the court released its formal charges for removal, suspended him with pay and coincidentally passed along to the Governor Yaccarino's application for disability retirement. The Chief Justice took the unusual step of advising the Governor that the court had determined to press ahead with the removal proceeding no matter what the Governor chose to do with the retirement application. This had the effect of delaying consideration of the disability matter. In short, the court advised the Executive that it intended to remove Yaccarino whether he was retired on disability or not.

This was certainly a curious posture, since the removal statute was written to protect the public from incompetent judges, not as a punitive sanction. If Yaccarino could have been retired, the entire removal proceeding would have been moot. The scene at the Chief Justice's office had obviously derailed our disability track, a conclusion evident by the court's failure to employ its own rules and accept Yaccarino's motion for removal for medical reasons, thereby avoiding the long, expensive and egregious removal proceedings. The rule specifically endorses medical incapacity as a cause of removal.

The Chief Justice and the court were bent on publicly excoriating Yaccarino. They chose to use the removal proceedings and other proceedings to vent their official spleens on one of their misbehaving palace guards.

Under the law, the Supreme Court may employ formal removal proceedings as an alternate to impeachment by the Legislature. The statute mandates a formal hearing by at least a three-judge panel established by the court. The hearing would then operate under special rules which had been proposed but had not been adopted at the time of the Yaccarino matter. So, we were subjected to more ad hoc procedures, that were of course approved by the court later.

The three judges selected by the Supreme Court for the hearing were Herman Michels, John Marzulli and Paul Lowengrub. Michels, a former civil litigation defense attorney and evident team player, had the type of personality which would never upset anyone. Marzulli had spent his entire judicial career toiling on the Essex Bench. He added the necessary ethnic balance. Lowengrub, a quiet, bookish scholarly type rounded out the panel. The balance was near perfect, as if their symmetrical selection had an eye to history.

The charges were detailed and massive and too burdensome for a single private practitioner. The defense team parceled out responsibilities. I remained 'lead counsel' (whatever that meant), responsible to defend the "dog/daughter" case. Joe Dempsey kept the judicial deportment cases. I asked Jack Ford, noted criminal defense attorney, to participate as counsel in defense of the "alcohol/bar" charges. Robert Del Tufo agreed to try the issue of the violation of the attorney/client privilege by Mr. Geiser.

Finally, we succeeded in securing Robert Novins to serve as counsel in the "house" case and to prepare the "medical" defense. Novins, a giant of a man both in physical stature and reputation, was a former judge. He gave a Herculean effort preparing a defense for what we felt, emotionally, was an indefensible case. My former partner at the time, Charles Uliano, served as utility man and backup for all of us. It was a thankless and difficult job, but he did it well.

The three-judge trial kicked off in a fashion illustrative of the folly of the whole process. The Administrative Office of the Courts, an arm of the Supreme Court, was supposed to be an impartial arbiter of the entire affair. They were caught handing out press releases in the court on the first day of hearings. The releases sought to explain and justify the proceedings against Yaccarino. When this breach of etiquette was brought to Judge Michels's attention, he 'respectfully' asked Assistant Attorney General Sullivan to call over and ask the A.O.C. to be a 'little more circumspect.' I found it infuriating that he was far more concerned with ruffling any feathers over there than he was to provide a professional and fair arbitration environment.

There was both humor and drama in the proceedings which dragged on over several weeks. Breathing a sigh of relief when they concluded, some on the defense team hoped our efforts had brought some overall enlightenment to the three judges. Maybe those three learned jurists would be able to see through the politics and publicity, get rational, and conclude Yaccarino's conduct was accounted for by medical and emotional conditions secondary to cardiac bypass surgery, and would therefore recommend he be removed for medical reasons or simply be permitted to retire. I didn't share that optimism and waited for the next "shoe to drop" in the tragedy.

Yaccarino's nemesis, the A.C.J.C. Chairman, had died. That very same day, the three-judge panel released its report which soundly condemned our client. Based on the report, the three judges had apparently tried an entirely different case and heard totally different evidence than heard by defense counsel. The reports contained comments on the judge's sharp intelligence and lucidity. Nothing could have been further from fact. At trial he looked and acted like Captain Queeg of "Caine Mutiny" fame. On at least one occasion while a witness, he objected to a question by the Attorney General and then sustained his own objection.

This report was released to the press and forwarded to the Supreme Court for its own action. We were invited to further brief the matter and then go on for oral argument. When the case was called for argument before the Supreme Court, we divided it up per our areas of responsibility. The court was not very responsive to any of our positions. It was especially interesting to watch Joe Dempsey argue the judicial deportment case. Joe has one of the most brilliant minds I have come across. His discussion and argument was on an intellectual plane that members of the court could not attain. Maybe out of insecurity, some Justices were rude to that fine appellate advocate.

One of the deportment cases concerned Yaccarino's comments from the bench to a divorced father who hadn't bothered to pursue visitation with his children for a while. When the father attempted to resume visitation, his ex-wife had objected.

Yaccarino castigated both sides and expounded his own beliefs on the parent-child relationship and divorce. He forcefully pointed out in allegorical terms how the bond was stronger than the legal system and holy in nature. During oral argument, Dempsey tried to point out how a trial judge can use strong allegorical references to make points relevant to the case and sophistication of the litigants.

His argument, as with all of our arguments, fell on deaf ears. The court was more concerned about how it looked to the public for a judge to use strong language or religiously-based words in a non-jury setting, not in striking a blow in favor of creativity, and true judicial freedom. Mere words expressed by a judge in an obvious effort to influence the future behavior of two stubborn, but intelligent litigants became a violation of the Code of Judicial Conduct. A great victory for mediocrity.

In the many months after argument and before decision, the court allowed us to supplement the record with medical treatises on the cardiac bypass phenomenon which we claimed affected Yaccarino's emotional and intellectual functioning. Medical science recognized a phenomenon of post-bypass psychosis or change due to insult to the brain during surgery.

Many problems were subtle. We produced overwhelming, credible evidence from fellow Monmouth County judges that after bypass surgery Yaccarino's behavior and personality became erratic and extreme.

The court's final opinion totally rejected any medical defense or alteration of accountability. Since the court's own rules recognized medical infirmity as a basis for removal it proved beyond question that the court was punishing Yaccarino and at the same time setting a dangerous standard for trial judges.

A more objective observer would have viewed those instances of extreme court behavior as supportive of our medical claims, and of the depth of Yaccarino's problem, not those of an individual who warranted a public flogging. But the factfinders were merely interested in the public perception of the whole affair, a reflection of the loss of humanity, mercy and empathy by our judicial brethren.

Shortly after Christmas 1985, the court issued its opinion, ending months of anxiety and Yaccarino's judicial career. He was immediately removed, and his salary stopped. *In re Yaccarino 101 N.J. 342 (1985)*.

It took the Office of the Governor another nine months to rule on his disability pension. The Governor himself wanted no part of that hot potato. He tossed it over to the State House Commission, and despite being the presiding officer of the Commission, managed to be out of town when our application came up for public consideration.

I had never been before the State House Commission which meets in a plushy carpeted office in the State House. Looking around, I thought I was in an English palace awaiting an audience with the King. There were courtesans everywhere and uniformed State Police appeared like the King's palace guard. People were constantly checking on who was there and who was speaking to whom. Quite a scene at that seat of power.

I was called in for our public hearing on the Yaccarino disability pension application. Acting Governor Senator John Russo was Chairman. The issue was simply whether the pension should be reduced by some percentage due to dishonorable service. I thought I would be functioning as a lawyer at the hearing; but instead, it was like negotiating the price of a used and damaged car. The Acting Governor brought these dramatic proceedings to a halt because he had a luncheon engagement.

So, after Yaccarino's public fall from grace, his humiliating removal with accompanying findings of misconduct, the coordinated branches of government, consisting of Legislative and Executive members, could agree such dishonesty justified only a seven and one-half per cent reduction of his pension. The Supreme Court had misused the removal mechanism to castigate a judge who simply wished to go on with his life outside of the judicial arena.

The persecution wasn't over. In 1986, the Office of Central Ethics, on its own, moved against Yaccarino's license to practice law, relying on the same activities used in the removal proceedings. The criminality of these same matters—or lack thereof—had been thoroughly investigated by the Attorney General, accompanied by the unusual grant of immunity to the very people Yaccarino claimed had conspired against him.

In the end, the Judge was prepared to disengage but the official "ego" of the court would not sit still to allow disengagement. The court needed a final frenzy of exorcising Yaccarino from its ranks. That came on Friday the 13th of December 1989 with his order of disbarment. *In re Yaccarino 117 N.J. 175 (1989).*

I had been the attorney for Thomas Yaccarino, individually and in association with several prominent attorneys, for some eight and one-half years. The saga started in April of 1981 and legally concluded in December 1989. Five Justices of the New Jersey Supreme Court completed the process which, for a myriad of reasons, sought to deprive an individual of his judgeship, his attorney's license and his dignity. Their perception of the "public interest" reeked of judicial tyranny similar to the historical leaders guilty of glories such as the Salem Witch Trials and the Spanish Inquisition. It became a personal tragedy to Thomas Yaccarino and his family, and a tragedy for—and failure of—the law.

The judgment of the court revealed fear: a fear to be human, a fear to feel, a fear to be just. Instead, the court was bent on doing what it saw as meeting some great public need.

The evidence submitted to the local Ethics Panel hearing the disbarment case, which consisted of highly seasoned, mature adults, convinced these lawyers that Thomas Yaccarino, at most, deserved a public reprimand. That evidence acknowledged that the personality change suffered by the judge as a result of the consequences of early heart bypass surgery had wreaked havoc on his sense of judgment and sense of propriety.

The uncontradicted evidence also demonstrated that, consistent with medical patterns of others, his medical condition had substantially improved and Yaccarino was a candidate for rehabilitation. This evidence was unavailable prior to the removal hearing. However, between the time of that hearing and the commencement of the Ethics hearings, we had secured substantial objective test results showing a dramatic improvement in his condition.

None of that mattered to the legal patricians who voted as the majority. The attorney presenting the case for the Office of Attorney Ethics didn't even rebut our evidence. He knew the die was cast. When the ethics case went on appeal to the Disciplinary Review Committee it was divided equally and produced two diametrically opposed and eloquent opinions—the only time that has occurred in New Jersey history.

So ended that legal odyssey of eight and one-half years. So ended the career of an individual who, notwithstanding his personality problems and dogmatic approach to reality, was probably the finest sentencing judge to serve in Monmouth County and one of the most pragmatic jurists to ever sit on the bench. He was also a pretty fair country lawyer.

From December 1989 to May 11, 1993 Tom Yaccarino attempted to restore the dignity improperly wrenched away from him by the court. Shortly before his death, his wife asked me to inquire about an application for re-admission to the bar. My request fell on deaf ears.

His mortal life finally ended, leaving behind a contrasting legacy of the astute, intelligent and practical legal decisions he rendered with the narrow, conformist, and vengeful policy of those against him dispensed by the very judiciary he loved.

That experience left me an outsider to the "establishment" forever.

State v. Curtis, 195 N.J. Super 354 (App. Div., 1984)

Two eighteen-year-olds, Scott Franz and Bruce Curtis, were charged with murdering Mr. and Mrs. Alfred Podgis in Loch Arbor, N.J.

I represented Bruce Curtis in the trial; he was acquitted of murder but convicted of aggravated manslaughter. The co-defendant pled guilty to murder and testified at the trial against Curtis on behalf of the State. Both were sentenced to 20 years and ineligible for parole for 10, the maximum sentence for a conviction of aggravated manslaughter.

Since the verdict, the case has received even more publicity than during trial. Allegations were raised that my client, a Canadian citizen, did not receive a fair trial. Media people have extensively looked into these allegations. I'm including the case here as it is illustrative of the pro-state bias found in trial judges who feel compelled to affect a particular result by way of trial, sentence or combination of both.

Curtis was charged with shooting Mrs. Podgis. Franz pled guilty to intentionally murdering his stepfather, Alfred Podgis. Their bodies were dumped off next to an interstate highway in rural Pennsylvania and the two killers drove first to the World's Fair in Tennessee and then on to Texas. They were apprehended when Franz used his stepfather's credit card. They were extradited to New Jersey to stand trial for murder and related offenses.

Curtis had grown up in a farm environment in Nova Scotia, Canada and was a stranger to firearms. At the trial, Franz claimed Curtis loaded a Winchester 30/30 with his own hands and brought it into the house. This may be why the jury convicted him of aggravated manslaughter. If the gun had accidentally gone off, where that gun had been intentionally brought into the house for a confrontation with a haywire adult, is that then aggravated manslaughter or traditional negligent manslaughter? There was a ten-year sentencing differential at stake.[6]

The Curtis trial judge listened attentively to the case and at some point, concluded that Curtis was guilty of murder. During a criminal trial, a trial judge has the last word with the jury. He provides it with a charge of the applicable law. This includes presentation of as many as a dozen major legal concepts.

The organization and content of the charge is basically left to his discretion. The manner of delivery, with emphasis, inflections, and facial or body language are all something a reviewing court cannot effectively analyze. All the appellate tribunal can check is whether the charge as written is legally acceptable.

This limited review is superficial and unless a charge is videotaped, there is little an advocate can do to challenge a trial judge's adroit effort to give a jury his own message. Jurors tend to look up to a trial judge. The message which comes across loud and clear to them may be hardly a whisper to the reviewing court.

I contended that the Curtis trial judge tailored his charge to make it essentially impossible to acquit the defendant of all charges and to push the jury toward murder, or aggravated manslaughter. Case in point, I'd discovered the judge in conference with an assistant prosecutor, *not* trial counsel, working up the charge without my input; a "charge conference" without the presence of the defense.

---

[6] The trial and the events underlying the death of the Podgis couple was the subject of a CBS made for television movie and at least one book "No Easy Answers".

One of the defense claims was that the shooting of Mrs. Podgis had occurred accidentally when Curtis was running out of the house and almost ran into Mrs. Podgis who suddenly came around a corner. We requested the court explain to the jury that accidental killing–which mandated an acquittal of all charges–was consistent with a finding of grossly negligent conduct and did not have to be blameless conduct. When pressed why the jury wasn't given this information, the court's answer was that the jury didn't ask.

It was clear to the court and counsel that the jury had to make a very adroit distinction as to level of culpability. The Criminal Code included definitions guiding a jury as to culpable conduct for purposes of judging conduct and selecting accidental non-criminal killing or the other three grades of criminal homicide. There was no question Curtis and Franz had taken loaded firearms into the Podgis house in the face of a rather explosive situation. Podgis was Franz's stepfather and had a serious history of proneness to violence and maintained nearly a dozen firearms in his home.

The concepts of aggravated manslaughter and manslaughter are very similar and difficult to distinguish. Yet, conviction of the first carries double the penalty of the other. The trial judge's explanation made it almost impossible to distinguish between the two and failed to explain to the jury the ultimate outcome of the jury's choice between them. The court refused to provide the legal definition of negligent killing which mandated acquittal of all homicide charges.

The jury knew codefendant Franz had pled guilty to murder, exposing him to a twenty-year maximum term with a ten-year parole ineligibility period. Hence, when the jury convicted Curtis of aggravated manslaughter, that jury was telling the court it didn't believe he was as culpable as Franz. Yet, at sentencing, Curtis was given the maximum sentence for aggravated manslaughter; the same sentence given to Franz for murder.

It is certainly an odd system for a jury's message to be totally ignored by the judges. Yet, this was precisely the net result in the Curtis case. Our jury system is the finest fact-finding mechanism in the world. Its mistakes and failures are generally attributable to intrusion of some external force. Unfortunately, and all too often, the intrusion comes from result-oriented trial judges.

The powerful trial judge, jaundiced in favor of the State and so-called public interest, was free to affect the outcome and then nail the door shut. What this judge and many others have forgotten is that public interest is best served by taking a truly neutral position and not becoming subjectively involved to affect a result. Though I doubt I'll see it in my time, someday, perhaps, more judges will embrace this thought.

Bruce Curtis was transferred to Canada to complete his sentence. His supporters succeeded in convincing New Jersey and the Federal Government to adopt a transfer act permitting that prisoner movement. He was released in early 1990. The net effect cut Curtis' time from twenty years to less than seven years behind bars, more akin to a manslaughter conviction then that of aggravated manslaughter.

What a strange twist of fate. Scott Franz was left behind with his half-truths to serve out his full sentence for murder, without parole. Bruce Curtis never told me or anyone else what happened on that hot July morning in Loch Arbor. One wonders whether Franz has the guts to tell the real truth when the only stake is just that: truth.

On appeal, the Appellate tribunal ignored my claim that the trial court should have explained to the jury that a person could be deemed grossly negligent in the use of a firearm and still not be guilty of simple manslaughter. It simply affirmed the conviction for aggravated manslaughter. So ended that case. I never spoke to the trial judge again.

This case marked the point in my career where I had had enough of trial judges directly intruding into high visibility cases to affect the outcome and then have, upon exposure, their design white-washed by our appellate courts.

I decided to largely transfer my efforts from criminal law to concentrate on major civil issues.

Kelly v. Gwinnell, 96 N.J. 538
(1984)

Of all the cases in which I have participated, Kelly v. Gwinnell probably gained the greatest notoriety. Our firm was retained by a severely injured motorist who had been struck head-on in her lane of travel by a drunk driver. Mrs. Kelly initiated suit against that driver; his lawyer filed a third-party complaint against the host/owners of a residence where the motorist had done his drinking shortly before the accident. We then joined those homeowners as direct defendants.

At that time in Monmouth County, motions for summary judgment were handled by two judges. Plaintiffs with last names beginning with A to M were handled by Judge Benedict Nicosia. Those with last names beginning with N to Z were handled by Judge Thomas Shebell. The defendant homeowners' attorney filed a motion for summary judgment against us and the driver, claiming that under the law they owed no duty to the motoring public regarding drinking in their private home. At that time, New Jersey had only one significant case on that subject, and it had dealt with the issue only indirectly. In Rappaport v. Nichols, 31 N.J. 188 (1959), the Supreme Court had decided a licensed liquor establishment could be liable to a patron and/or third party if it had served alcohol to its patron who it knew or should have known was visually intoxicated.

At approximately the same time the motion was filed against us, another defendant in a similar case filed a similar motion. That matter was assigned to Judge Shebell and ours assigned to Judge Nicosia. Several weeks before our matter was to be heard, Judge Shebell issued an opinion concluding that the homeowner could be liable, and the case could go to a trial by jury. Eventually that case settled.

Notwithstanding Judge Shebell's opinion and the other precedent, Judge Nicosia held there was no duty from a homeowner to the traveling public. He concluded if one went to another's home, was served alcohol to the point of extreme drunkenness, then smashed into another vehicle on a public highway, the homeowner could not be liable to the innocent and injured motorist.

The concept of "duty" is a·form of judicial censorship. As a preliminary matter, a judge has the right to dismiss a private tort claim for damages if he determines one individual has no legal duty to another under a given set of circumstances. This finding is based on some vague concept or the presence of a positive social policy. In the Freehold courthouse, within a few months, two judges looking at the same set of circumstances had reached opposite conclusions on what was good or bad social policy.

One concluded an adult host owed no duty to third persons regarding excessive drinking in their home by a guest. Another concluded just the opposite. This procedure tends to run afoul of basic expectations of the right to a determination of such questions by a jury. Though no one elected the judge, the judiciary seized the power to determine the duty question. Where the legislature has not spoken, such issues are uniquely suited for determination by a group of citizens. Social policy should not be set by a judge, absent legislative pronouncement on the subject.

At this point there remained the claim of plaintiff versus the drunken driver. In this posture, there was no right to an appeal from Judge Nicosia's action without permission of the appellate court, unless the trial judge certified the ruling as equivalent to a final judgment, or until the remaining case was concluded. This Court Rule of Procedure was adopted to cut down on the volume of appeals based on the assumption that many such appeals simply die once the remaining parties disposed of their claims.

In reality and practice, the rule is an abomination. At best it prolongs the litigation, proliferates jury trials, causes extensive duplication of effort and makes it extremely expensive and time consuming to properly litigate serious questions in our courts. Interestingly, there is a serious movement to eliminate from the rule, any right of the trial judge to certify the matter as final judgment. The most recent Court Rule considerably cuts down this right. *See Rule 4:42-2*. Our appeals courts go out of their way to avoid what they consider piecemeal Appellate review.

I handled another case in which an appellate court dismissed our appeal after a full briefing of the issues and oral argument, concluding that the trial judge should simply have not certified the matter as final under the rule. Imagine having to explain that delay and waste to our client.

It sometimes seems our courts go out of their way making access to them impractical, time-consuming and full of landmines and traps. The costs of preparing an appeal and then having it dismissed are astronomical. Obviously, there are motions which shouldn't be appealed. However, when a party has a claim against multiple defendants, that claim may be simplified by the filing of a motion for partial summary judgment by one of those defendants. Under the existing rule, it is necessary to try the case against the remaining defendants before you may safely appeal from a dismissal of the claim against the one defendant let out early without a trial. Common sense would dictate that you have a right of appeal on the question of the right to a trial against the one defendant before having to try the balance of the case against the remaining defendants. The present rule is an unworkable anachronism and creates delay and uncertainty in an already under- performing system.

We were fortunate Judge Nicosia certified the dismissal as a final judgment. Even more oddly fortunate, the judges of the appellate court were incensed enough against our claim not to avail themselves of dismissing our appeal after argument. Instead they wished to use the case to write an opinion clearly establishing complete non-liability of homeowners and did so in the strongest of terms. 190 N.J. Super 320 (App. Div .1983).

Oral argument was a huge personal disappointment for me. The three judges took turns attacking our claim as if we were jeopardizing their own cocktail party practices and drinking style. Their attitude would discourage anyone from raising a novel issue or pressing some generally unpopular idea. While the common law presupposes an evolvement of theory and thought, the three judges in Kelly were uncommonly rigid in their positions.

That attitude prevails in our justice system. Judges feel overwhelmed by the sheer volume of cases confronting them, so developments in the common law are stunted. The volume leads to less opinions being written, with less explanation, more per curiams issued, less argument granted and the absence of reasoned dissents. Judges generally prefer not to be asked to decide any serious questions of law. The stimulating intellectual techniques taught in every law school in the country get discarded in the practice. We're all too busy "moving cases" to properly deal with real questions, tough questions raised in our modern society.

The statistics are shocking: During the period September 1, 2012 through August 31, 2013 our Appellate Division issued 3,121 opinions. Of these, only 158 were officially published. See my comments about State v. Miller, 220 N.J. Super. 106 (App. Div. 1985) for discussion of this abuse. Of the published opinions there were a grand total of two dissents. Out of all 3,121 opinions, there were only five dissents. When a dissent is filed, there is a right to appeal to the State Supreme Court.

Proper, full treatment is still available in some cases, like Kelly, but only when somebody on the court has his interest piqued. We were all taught to state a cogent and a clearly prepared argument of persuasion when perfecting an appeal. Now we have an additional condition to meet: stimulate a judge's law secretary and then the judge to get them into the matter. Otherwise, expect boiler plate responses and short shrift treatment. All who've appeared at oral argument have suffered the sinking feeling of knowing only one panel member was truly ready for argument. This volume-induced malaise is truly shameful.

After receiving the Appellate Division opinion rejecting our claim, our firm seriously considered abandoning any further appeal of the case against the homeowner, though based on the facts, Kelly cried out for a finding of some responsibility by the homeowners for their contribution in putting a person in the driver's seat unfit to operate a car on the public highway. The blood alcohol reading of the drunken motorist had been extremely high; he had done all his imbibing at the house of the co-defendants with them at a kitchen table. The host, concerned for the guest's obviously drunken condition, had called his home to see if he made it home.

The trial of the case against the driver had been held up more than a year to allow the parties to perfect the appeal from Judge Nicosia's ruling. Now we had to look at a "Petition for Certification" to the New Jersey Supreme Court, a document arguing why the court ought to exercise its discretionary review of our appeal. If the court decided to take the case, we would be permitted to orally argue to the full Supreme Court. An affirmative vote of three justices was required to obtain such full review. The process could take as little as six months and as much as eighteen months. We were not convinced our chances of success warranted the investment of this additional time and effort. However, the plaintiff's injuries would probably exceed the full amount of the liability insurance policy of the defendant driver. The insurer, too, was interested in pursuing their crossclaim against the hosts in the Supreme Court. We made the decision to proceed, using our firm's best writer to draft our Petition.

Several months later we received word that the Supreme Court of New Jersey had decided to take the case for full review. An argument date was established, and I began to prepare for my appearance. This time the oral argument would not be in a hostile environment, as it had been in the Appellate Division.

Instead, the court was very interested in our reasoning to support the claim, and of how the precedents, both within and without of New Jersey, affected that reasoning. The court was also concerned with some very practical effects of a favorable ruling on social activities, cost of insurance coverage and the question of whether liability coverage was even available. It was an invigorating experience to appear in this court for our client. It is a shame every appearance in the appellate courts is not of similar caliber. One gets the feeling that the quality of the performance is proportionate to the level of interest of the individual judges or justices.

On June 27, 1984, my birthday, the court issued its opinion. By a six to one majority it decided that, henceforth, a host at a private home could be found at least partially responsible if (1) that host served alcohol to a visibly intoxicated guest; who (2) the host knew was going to operate a motor vehicle; and (3) that guest then caused injury to an innocent third party in an automobile accident. In short, the court found a duty running from a private host to third parties in automobiles on our streets and highways. It extended the logic in Linn v. Rand, 140 N.J. Super. 212 (App. Div. 1976) as on point and worth extending, stating:

There, practically all of the considerations urged here against liability were present: it was a social setting at someone's home, not at a tavern; the one who provided the liquor to the intoxicated minor was a host, not a licensee; and all of the notions of fault and causation pinning sole responsibility on the drinker were present.

The only difference was that the guest was a minor but whether obviously so or whether known to the host is not disclosed in the opinion. Kelly at 547.

That finding unleashed a fire storm of public outcry and criticism. Our Supreme Court had now trifled with the partying and drinking habits of the citizens of New Jersey.

On the day following the decision, I returned to my office in West Long Branch from court in Freehold and discovered it had been invaded by news people, including TV cameras from CBS and ABC News. My senior partner, George M. Chamlin, was already basking in the light of public exposure. In fairness to him, the plaintiff was originally his client.

Calls from commentators and news people came from all over the country. My partner and I appeared on several news and personality shows in New York and Philadelphia. The issue of host liability unleashed diametrically opposed views. MADD–Mothers Against Drunk Driving, was ecstatic. Certain New Jersey senators called for impeachment of Chief Justice Wilentz. His authoring the majority opinion was considered a factor against his controversial tenure appointment a few years later.

Looking back on the decision, it appears to have been much ado about insignificant numbers of matters. In thirty years since the decision, there probably haven't been 1000 actual cases started as a result of that new duty of care. The decision criticized by some as overbroad had a positive effect, sensitizing people about the problem of drunk driving and perhaps making those at private social gatherings, think just a little before taking that extra drink and then "hitting" the road.

As a matter of social policy, and as an example of common law keeping up with the times, the decision was a good one. The resulting criticism of the court was far out of proportion and in certain respects, totally unwarranted. People with an "axe to grind" against the court or some of its Justices used the case to stimulate some unthinking and selfish attitudes. The legislature, where certain of its members are still Neanderthal in their thinking, sought to pass a law to upset and/or seriously delimit the duty. Instead, the bill which became law codified the Kelly decision. Those seeking to upset the decision were defeated, though the statute did severely limit further expansion of the host's liability doctrine.

The court remanded the case back to Monmouth County to be disposed of with the rest of the matter. When the trial came up, my partner basked in the limelight and then settled the whole case within the combined policy dollar limits of the insurance carriers of the host and the drunken driver. I always wondered why, after the win in the Appellate Division, the liability carrier for the host didn't call us up and settle the claim for a lot less, thereby leaving rejection of host liability as the law in the state.

What has stayed with me over the years is this question: In the absence of statutory law, why is major social policy left to the personal attitudes and biases of unelected judges instead of a group of citizens called a jury?

I suggest this occurs because of the abysmal failure of our so-called two-party system to act on the basis of right, not the self-interest of industry groups. Social policy is set by courts only when the legislature has failed to act to meet a problem identified in litigation. History is replete with such actions.

The "one man, one vote" decisions of the U.S. Supreme Court came down only after warnings by the court that it would fashion a judge-made remedy if the states didn't deal with the problem. *See Baker v. Carr, 369 U.S. 186, 82 S. Ct. 691, 7 L.Ed.2d 663 (1962) and its progeny.*

Likewise, the search and seizure "exclusionary rule" of Mapp v. Ohio, 367 U.S. 643, 81 S. Ct. 1684, 6 L.Ed.2d 1081 (1961) was fashioned by the Supreme Court after the states ignored its warning, as found in Wolf v. Colorado, 338 U.S. 25, 69 S. Ct. 1359, 93 L. Ed. 1782- (1949).

'Duty,' as defined by courts, should be resolved by citizen juries. Who better to judge their own behavior? Maybe that day will come. The Kelly experience was enlightening in its approach, the kind of case that keeps real advocates plowing ahead, hoping they'll someday get another one.

It's a good lesson for those attorneys committed to making the common law contribute to the common good. While we can hope members of the bench rule creatively and responsibly, individual citizens empaneled as a jury are best at measuring duty as an extension of the social compact. The legislature is second choice; judges, last. As some of the following cases point out, there are recognized criteria used by the court to extend a legal duty. Just as easily as judges, juries could apply those criteria to the duty question.

Herman v. Sunshine Specialties, 257 N.J. Super 533 (App. Div., 1992) Rev. 133 N.J. 329 (1993)

When an action includes claims for both compensatory and punitive damages—and a liability policy is available to the defendant—defending clients can get very messy. New Jersey law has long held a defendant ordinarily cannot purchase liability insurance to cover punitive damages. When these claims are made, many attorneys counsel the defense client to retain a second lawyer. Unfortunately, the defense lawyer in this case chose not to tell Sunshine Chemicals to do so. As a result, we had a second claim to collect all the monies awarded by the jury.

The case started out as a products liability claim against the manufacturer of a bathroom spray used in small closed-in areas to clean and disinfect tiles, usually residential or office bathrooms. My client claimed to have suffered an aggravation of her allergy and asthmatic condition through exposure to the stuff. Discovery revealed the manufacturer had enough information to properly label the product with appropriate warnings. Instead, they intentionally deleted the warnings and used a totally benign warning. Consequently, we amended our complaint to include a claim for punitive damages.

When the case first came on for trial, the defense attorney, a well- respected and experienced trial lawyer, made no offer to settle. However, after the company president did rather poorly on cross-examination the liability carrier offered $400,000 in settlement. We countered with a $500,000 demand. The liability carrier would not budge, and the defense lawyer never called the president of the company who had testified the day before to see if the company would contribute $100,000 to our settlement demand.

The case went to the jury for both claims of compensatory and punitive damages. It returned with a verdict of $400,000 compensatory and $400,000 punitive damages. The carrier almost immediately paid the compensatory portion, but at the direction of its client, filed an appeal of the punitive damage awarded.

On appeal, the issue for the court was whether the amount of the punitive award had to bear some relationship to the "net worth" of the defendant and if so, how that should be calculated. There was evidence the defendant's business had been sold for a net of $750,000 a year or two after the accident. The Appellate Division felt the sales value of the business was an inadequate yard stick and we had to do a full analysis of the true "net worth" at the time of the plaintiff's claim to properly set any punitive damage award.

In the court's view, how much a tortfeasor stood to lose as a result of its glaring misconduct, was simply a function of its "net worth." This overly technical and legislative approach seemed to say punitive damages were a bookkeeping function when it came to corporations and businesses.

I applied to the New Jersey Supreme Court for review and was granted the opportunity to have the issue determined by our high court. Sure enough, the court applied some common sense, thereby explaining "net worth" is not the total delimiting factor, but only one of the circumstances to be considered by a jury in deciding what amount of punitive damages was enough to punish a civil wrongdoer.

The court established the procedure to follow in cases where there were claims for both compensatory and punitive damages and reinstated our verdict of $400,000 for punitive damages. That action was extremely unusual. It appeared to be aimed at the defense council's handling of the entire issue.

That decision provoked a second case, as the carrier ordinarily would not voluntarily pay a punitive damage verdict and the defendant company was defunct by the time of the New Jersey Supreme Court opinion. I had to start another suit against both the defendant's insurance carrier and its trial attorney. Under the law, a carrier has the duty, as does the lawyer, to do what it can to protect the insured from exposure to a jury verdict not covered by its insurance, such as punitive damages. Here, both insurance company and lawyer had failed to advise the defendant company of the settlement opportunity and give it the chance to offer to pay the $100,000 spread between our demand and the carrier's last offer. I never knew what my client would have done if we were offered $50,000 over the carrier's $400,000 offer.

After we filed our complaint and issue was joined, the carrier for the defendant Company and its former trial lawyer's carrier asked to mediate our claim. Such intervention by a private retired judge is an expeditious way to end a case prior to paying large amounts to defend essentially indefensible ones.

After the mediator recommended defendants pay the award, they acquiesced, and the plaintiff received the other $400,000 in damages.

The Herman case remains the leading New Jersey standard on how to try a combined compensatory and punitive damage civil case. The entire litigation from the initial suit through settlement took in excess of seven years. After the decision, the NJ Legislature codified the law in a statute.

Ahn v. Kim, 145 N.J. 246
(1996)

Another weird story is of a case that came to me in 1985. The wife of an anesthesiologist had suffered the actual "loss" of her husband, Dr. Ahn, the day after his admission to the Carrier Foundation, a well-known psychiatric hospital in Belle Mead, New Jersey.

Dr. Ahn had been suffering severe and debilitating depression and was taken to this mental hospital for inpatient care. He was placed in an unlocked "open unit" and simply disappeared the night of his admission. When he couldn't be located on the grounds, a widespread search was conducted over a large area of a very rural section of New Jersey. He was never found. We were retained to bring a claim for the negligence of the institution, some of its nurses and others in placing him in an unguarded and open wing after his initial intake. However, we first had to get a "declaration of death." In New Jersey it required six years of never seeing or hearing from him—and obviously not recovering a body. The court finally declared Dr. Ahn dead in 1991.

We then filed a wrongful death action on behalf of his estate. Under the law, damages were circumscribed by the pecuniary loss to the decedent's estate. In addition, when suing a hospital, there was a $10,000 cap on recovery unless you could identify a named employee of the hospital and prove that person's fault. Later that cap was significantly increased to $250,000—but well after the conclusion of our case. We sued the hospital, the admitting psychiatrist and two nurses. The case eventually came on for jury trial before an undistinguished and lazy trial judge at the Ocean County Court house. The defense was represented by some highly distinguished trial attorneys, and the issues were rather novel and quite complex.

Unfortunately, the trial judge simply followed the defense lead and ruled against the plaintiff on all the issues. When this confusing case was presented to a jury, they voted 6 to 2 against any defendant negligence. After over seven years of effort the widow and her two children were left with nothing.

We appealed the defense judgment to the Superior Court Appellate Division. Our appeal brief contended the trial judge had made a "shambles of the trial." The appellate court agreed, reversing the judgment and sending the case back for retrial. However, that opinion still restricted us from the benefit of the presumption of death after more than six years of Dr. Ahn's unaccountedness.

This was critical to our proof of death, since the defense was arguing Mrs. Ahn's husband might have fled back to North Korea, where he had been born. The Supreme Court granted both ours and the defendants' request for review. It agreed we could rely on the presumption of death resulting from the judicial declaration of death and the defense could not rely on the presumption against suicide at the retrial.

We had a different judge at retrial, and we prevailed. The jury, which was not told about the $10,000 cap limitation awarded $2.5 million, apportioning fault between the two named nurses and security at the institution.

Since we had not identified any named individual for breach of security, the security portion of the jury verdict was reduced to the cap of $10,000 plus the amount reflecting the negligence of two named nurses, so the final verdict was reduced to slightly more than $1,000,000, plus interest and costs.

Both sides appealed the decision. We'd argued the jury should be told of the effect of the cap on a possible award. The defense had also made some serious motions, denied at trial. On February 23, 1999, the Appellate Division issued a 97-page opinion, unpublished, affirming the entire decision and leaving me with a very frustrated client. The jury had found significant institutional responsibility, but its will was thwarted because we couldn't identify specific, negligent institutional employees.

It had taken fourteen years, two jury trials, one Supreme Court opinion and two Appellate Division opinions to conclude the litigation. Even without the six year wait to obtain a declaration of death, it took eight plus years to resolve the case.

To use an old adage, justice delayed is justice denied.

Security Cases

Clohesy v. Food Circus Supermarkets, Inc. 149 N.J. 496 (1997)
and
X. v. Route 37 Shopping Center

Clohesy was my next visit to the New Jersey Supreme Court. A retired schoolteacher went to shop at the Food Circus, a large store located on Broad Street in Red Bank, New Jersey. It had a big parking lot, without any external security and the operator simply ignored whatever went on outside the store enclosure.

In the middle of the afternoon, the victim exited her vehicle and was immediately accosted by an individual who, shortly before, had been discharged from a psychiatric unit at Riverview Medical Center. He forced her into her own car, drove away, and at some point, murdered her.

I got the case and conducted an extensive investigation to determine if there was much of a history of crime in the area or at the defendant facility. The defendant insisted there had been no prior car-jackings or similar events at its parking lot. The trial judge–the same judge from S. v. Curtis, concluded that the proprietor was entitled to one free carjacking before the duty of any security arose. Summary judgment was granted, and the case dismissed.

Off we went to the appellate division for review. The one free hi- jacking had charm for this panel as well. There is a right to appeal to the New Jersey Supreme Court if there is a dissent in the appellate division. Fortunately, one judge had dissented. We therefore appealed to the Supreme Court.

Justice Coleman, he of the enlightened trial bench in S. V. Vinegra, wrote an opinion with national implications. He opined that one free hi-jacking was not dispositive of this duty on proprietors of large stores, but merely one factor with others in determining liability for failure to provide any outside security. Any time you go to a mall, or large shopping area, and see those security vehicles or the security cameras, you can smile and take your hat off to the New Jersey Supreme Court for its positive social policy analysis. The common law at its zenith.

The extensive use of security cameras and outside security emanated from the Clohesy opinion, which notified mall owners and proprietors of large stores with major parking facilities that there was a duty to protect patrons from predators preying on them in their parking lots and facilities. An entire cottage industry was stimulated by Justice Coleman's reasoning.

After the decision, the case settled for a modest amount of money when plaintiff's circumstances were weighed under the New Jersey Wrongful Death Statute, a 1951 law which unfairly limits death claims under 18th century terms. An enlightened law was vetoed by Governor Corzine.

After Clohesy, other counsel retained me to work with them on another abduction case coming from the Route 37 Shopping Center in Toms River, New Jersey.

I have not used the name of the victim or her husband since the case was settled under a confidentiality covenant.

Mrs. X went into a Route 37 shopping center in Toms River, New Jersey in the middle of the afternoon. This Center operator hadn't heard of the Clohesy opinion and offered no security to or for protection of its patrons. When you exited the store, you were on your own.

A young man decided he liked her motor vehicle and wanted it for his upcoming birthday. He seized her and her vehicle in broad daylight. As he drove away, she desperately tried to convince him not to harm her. We know this because the teacher secretly taped it on a recorder in her pocketbook. Instead, he suffocated her in a barren section of Toms River. The criminal case achieved national attention when the tape was discovered in her pocketbook which was left at the murder scene.

We hired one Norman Bates, the leading expert on shopping center security in the country. We then conducted our discovery.

In preparing our civil case, we sought to interview the killer, then housed in Trenton State Prison under a guilty plea arranged by his public defender. We were shocked to discover an intelligent, soft spoken youth, someone entirely out of sync with who we thought we would find.

This stimulated me to obtain the prosecutor's file as part of my discovery in the civil case. In New Jersey, if a minor (under age 18) commits a serious crime the prosecutor can ask the court for permission to try the defendant as an adult. The court weighs the situation and makes the call.

Here, the public defender had secured the evaluation of a well-qualified expert opining the youth was operating with an unusual set of mental problems, at least in part from being struck in the head with a baseball bat. For inexplicable reasons, this expert had not been called during the hearing to determine if the youth should have been tried as an adult. That finding would either expose the youth to a limited incarceration as a youthful offender or life in prison as an adult criminal. Without offering the court any defense other than his youth and no prior juvenile record, that court ordered the seventeen-year-old to be tried as an adult. A plea deal was completed shortly afterward, and the defendant received a 30-year sentence in state prison.

I contacted that expert. If we tried our civil case, I reasoned that I might need his testimony to show the degree of *mens rea* of the youth to be contrasted with the conduct of the negligence of the shopping center defendant. The courts have ruled juries trying this type of civil case need to do a comparative fault analysis. Contrasting an intentional act with simple negligence is not an easy task.

When I called this expert, he first thought I was a public defender, since he'd never heard from them after submitting his report. When we realized what he had concluded about the youth's mental condition and the fact that his conclusions and opinion had not been made known to the court, it brought into focus the monstrous failure of the public defender system.

We then found out the youth was given a new trial because his public defender lawyer was having an affair with the young man's mother and had used her to influence the entry of his guilty plea.

When a different public defender tried the case, the defendant was convicted and sentenced to more time than the guilty plea had yielded to him. Again, no effort was made to use the expert to mitigate the crime, the sentence or the fact that the first court should have reconsidered the decision to try him as an adult.

You really cannot make this stuff up.

Meanwhile, we obtained a handsome settlement from the mall operator with which the widower and his child put their lives back together. The youthful killer sits in Trenton State Prison.

Perhaps, he has become the second victim. He is clearly a victim of an incompetent system. The psychologist is still awaiting a call from a non-existent lawyer for the defendant which will never come.

Campione v. Soden, 150 N.J. 163 (1997)

This garden variety auto-negligence case turned into a major claim under our court rules, both procedurally and substantially.

The plaintiff was a passenger in a motor vehicle stopped at a traffic light when it was struck from behind. After exiting the vehicle to examine the rear of the car, the vehicle that had struck his vehicle was itself struck from behind by another car, propelling it into the host vehicle again. The plaintiff's legs were pinned between the car at the right corner of his vehicle.

In the second impact he suffered severe and objective injuries to both legs. A combination of the two accidents caused him to suffer neck and back injuries along with some additional head and emotional trauma. The three drivers were named as defendants and the trial became a long one as the parties could not agree on the question of damages let alone apportioning them between the two impacts.

In civil trials, the court prepares a set of questions to be submitted to the jury to aid them in their deliberations. Here, counsel were given only five to ten minutes to review the jury questions the court had drawn up at the conclusion of the multi-week trial. The jury returned a verdict of $750,000 for the plaintiff against the two operators of the rear-ending vehicles. When we reviewed the answers to prepare an appropriate judgment, we discovered one of the questions created an ambiguity on how much each defendant had to pay.

We filed a motion under a section of Rule 4:39-1 which allows a trial judge to make supplemental findings after a jury's verdict to carry out the jury's intention. This rule is seldom invoked. However, the trial judge used common sense and supplemented the jury verdict, allowing us to enter a judgment that, we thought, would resolve the case.

One of the offended defendants took an appeal to the Appellate Division and won a partial retrial on damages. Not satisfied with a partial victory, that defendant filed a petition for certification to the New Jersey Supreme Court. We were unhappy with having to retry any portion of the case, so we also petitioned the court to review the partial retrial portion of the decision. The court granted the defendant's petition but denied ours.

At oral argument the court realized a fair review of even the defendant's portion of the matter required review of our corresponding cross-petition. In an unprecedented move, the court retroactively granted our petition, reversed the Appellate Division and reinstated the trial court's finding of the supplemental missing facts. It directed the defendants to pay the original judgment.

This represented a stunning turn-around for plaintiff's side and distinguished the court in demonstrating how it could change its mind, act in a practical way and construe its own rules in a flexible manner.

For me, this opinion represented a high-water mark for Supreme Court adjudicatory actions, approximately 180 degrees from its behavior in the second In re Yaccarino opinion.

In Campione, the court demonstrated an informed and insightful approach to its rules, the substantive law and a difficult circumstance. Eight years before, in the second Yaccarino case, the same Court acted arbitrarily by disbarring Judge T. L. Yaccarino without permitting argument, simply invoking *res judicata* and ignoring the findings of an ethics panel of seasoned attorneys and four members of its own appellate committee.

The conclusion I've drawn? The personality of the high court changes based on the nature of the dispute and the questions it must resolve. There is a class of civil cases, such as Kelly, Herman, Ahn, Campione, and Clohesy where the perception of the court was more open and objective.

However, where certain matters directly involve the court, such as in Yaccarino, it adopts an almost hostile attitude and loses its objectiveness. As a litigator, at oral argument in both types of cases, I can see this serious dichotomy.

Where the issues do not implicate certain governmental or political options, the court can be open minded and act for the general good. Where the issues directly impact the court's own territory or structure, it acts subjectively and at times unjustly or even politically.

In Yaccarino, where one of its own had acted and kept acting out of sync with what powerful people felt was appropriate, there was no stopping the train from rolling over him and his interests.

Quite the contrary in Kelly, Clohesy, Herman, Ahn, and Campione.

Thank heaven for an objective search for justice.

The Racing Cases

During the middle years, I developed an interest in cases arising out of harness racing situations, usually where a trainer/driver was involved with alleged drugging of horses, or drugs found in the stables.

The usual order of adjudication was (1) an administrative law judge, (2) the New Jersey Racing Commission (NJRC), followed by (3) an appellate court. Like in the teacher cases, I could usually get some procedural help from these appellate judges, but rarely any substantive adjudication in favor of the horsemen.

In my opinion, the NJRC has disgraced itself as an agency devoid of fairness, doing only what is politically correct. A typical example of this is when a horse tests positive for a foreign substance. The NJRC rules provide a hearing mechanism for the affected trainer: if the NJRC finds the testing procedure was proper, the horse's trainer is strictly liable. Though the NJRC has never adopted a set of penalties, the stewards will generally impose a suspension. The trainer will decide to voluntarily accept that suspension or appeal it.

If appealed, the NJRC's Executive Director must consider a stay of penalty during the appeal process. If the Executive Director likes the trainer, he grants the appeal; if he doesn't, he doesn't. Appeals can often take longer than the original suspension. To protect the process and not allow it to become moot, an application must be made to the Superior Court, Appellate

Division for a stay pending completion of the Administrative Appeal process. Like everything involved with horse racing the whole process is very expensive and time consuming and only a certain few can afford it.

Neither the NJRC or the courts have set up meaningful written standards governing stay requests, so it is typically left to the subjective judgement of the Executive Director and/ or the Appellate judges.

In February 1988, Tom Luchento's barn was raided and a refrigerator there was found to contain several types of medication and drugs. Charges were filed and the Executive Director refused a stay even though Luchento's veterinarian claimed to be the owner of the alleged contraband. So off I went to the Superior Court Appellate Division. After an emergency Appellate argument with a full panel of the court, the following order was entered:

"Leave to Appeal is granted. We summarily reverse and order a stay of enforcement of the indefinite suspension pending administrative review."

Ultimately a settlement was worked out with a relatively short suspension and fine. This occurred over a year later. If the court had not acted, my client would have been forced to serve a longer suspension and would have lost his livelihood.

State v. Turcotte, 1989

Three months later, I was back in a similar situation with Ron and Lisa Turcotte, a husband and wife team who were both licensed harness trainers.

They owned a farm in Englishtown, New Jersey. When one of their horses tested positive, the New Jersey State Police, without a search warrant, entered the Turcotte's private stable area and found syringes and medications.

The Turcottes were criminally charged and their licenses suspended indefinitely. The same NJRC Executive Director, in tyrannical fashion, refused to issue a stay though there were substantial issues that needed resolution, including Fourth Amendment claims of first impression.

Back I went for an emergency appearance before a different panel of the Superior Court, Appellate Division. Different panel, same result:

"Leave to Appeal is granted. We summarily reverse the Racing Commission's (Executive Director) denial of a stay. Enforcement of the indefinite suspension is stayed pending review by the racing commission."

The administrative case on licensure was held up while we litigated the search and seizure of the syringes and medication. The opinion, in State v. Turcotte 239 N.J. Super 285 (App. Div., 1990) had national Fourth Amendment implications. The court upheld the right to search a private farm without a search warrant when a horse had tested positive, likening it to a mere administrative search—a recognized exception to the warrant requirement. It also believed less constitutional protection should be afforded as harness racing needed to be highly regulated because of its pari-mutuel betting.

Meanwhile, another lawyer, not associated with my firm, tried the disorderly persons charges in Englishtown Municipal Court. The Turcottes were convicted of illegal possession of the syringes and medications. I took the appeal for them to the Superior Court, Law Division. The trial judge acquitted the Turcottes of the syringe charge but convicted them of possession of unlawful legend drugs. On behalf of the Turcottes I then took the case back on appeal for my third appearance in the Superior Court, Appellate Division.

On October 1, 1991 that court took the unusual step of acquitting the Turcottes in an unreported opinion filed that date. The administrative charges against Mrs. Turcotte were later dropped, and Mr. Turcotte received a 90-day suspension of his trainer's license. That chapter was complete. If the original panel of the Appellate Division had refused the stay, the Turcottes would have taken a substantial penalty and probably lost their farm.

Interestingly, the Committee on Opinions opted not to publish the October 1, 1991 opinion, even though it had made law in acquitting them and it had published the search and seizure case. A strange use of publication options.

Pelling – case

The following year, I was back before another panel of the Appellate Division for another very successful trainer, Brett Pelling. As with Luchento and Turcotte, a search of Pelling's farm produced syringes and medications. This time the State Police did not file criminal charges. Instead, the NJRC suspended his license indefinitely and the Executive Director, of course, denied a stay.

Back to the Superior Court, Appellate Division. After a full briefing of our motion and the Deputy Attorney General's opposition, on January 23, 1989 the court stated:

"Leave to appeal is granted and the Commission's (Executive Director) denial of a stay pending Appeal to it is reversed. The indefinite suspension is stayed pending Appeal to the racing commission."

Approximately six months later the matter was resolved with a suspension for Mr. Pelling of sixty days.

Not once during that triple header did or would the court consider sanctions against the Executive Director, or issue a formal written opinion requiring him to grant stays pending Administrative review, which generally took from 18 months to two years until the NJRC's final decision.

This legal quirk continues to this day, as evidenced by the Dream with Me Stable case, discussed in the 21st Century section of this book.

Through his actions, the NJRC Executive Director has become the imperial czar of New Jersey Racing discipline cases. If you can't get a stay, you have no leverage and must simply cave to the demand for punishment which far exceeds the bounds of reasonableness.

Another example: the case of David MacNeill v. New Jersey Racing Commission, A-3919096T2. The trainer made the mistake of representing himself before the Commission which, after imposing a six-month suspension based on the suggestion of one of its investigators, felt sorry for the licensee. It, not the Executive Director, granted a stay pending my appeal to the Appellate Division.

Sure enough, on review of the matter, that court concluded the suspension was improper and remanded the case back to the Commission to act with reason.

On remand, the licensee worked out a much shorter penalty. If he had not received a stay, by the time the court reviewed the suspension at least six months or more would have passed. To get the stay from the Appellate Court after Administrative adjudication and denial by the agency, is almost impossible as the court standard is practically impossible to make.

The stay procedure in the Court rules is vague and needs revamping. Yet for more than thirty years, the Courts have refused to set written rules for the standard to determine when to grant a stay on an appeal from actions interlocutory by an administrative agency.

Devitis v. New Jersey Racing Commission, 202 N.J. Super 484 (App. Div., 1985)

In Devitis, the appellate court upheld a penalty to a driver who allegedly failed to make a proper effort to win a harness race. All races are taped. After the race in question, the track had a major fire destroying the grandstand and the race tape. Even though there was no hard evidence, the Racing Judges and State Steward were permitted to give their opinions.

Without access to the tape, there was no way to effectively question the subjective opinion of the officials. This is no different from where the State claims someone was in possession of marijuana and loses the evidence. It has nothing but the subjective opinion of an officer who thought it was marijuana.

In Devitis, our appellate court okayed a suspension based on the subjective opinion the driver was not trying to win the race. I challenged this procedure and my arguments were rejected by the court, in a reported opinion. New Jersey has a "net option" rule. Such opinions are not admitted to evidence except when such opinions are needed to penalize a harness racing driver.

King v. New Jersey Racing Commission, 103 N.J. 412 (1986)

King followed Devitis. Once again, a court found it comfortable to bend over backwards to allow the New Jersey Racing Commission to have its way. Jim King was cited by the judges for not winning a race that officials thought he should have won.

During the hearing before the State Steward, he was handed a severe, nine-month suspension. Our appeal was referred over to the Office of Administrative Law to conduct a "due process" hearing. On review of the race tape, several prominent drivers testified that in their opinion, King's horse was going on a break[7] shortly before the finish line. King had to get the horse on gait, rather than allow it to run through the finish line.

The Administrative Law judge, who heard the testimony of both Commission officials and those appearing on King's behalf, reviewed the tape himself, concluded there had been no violation. He directed King be found not guilty of an improper drive.

The case went back to the New Jersey Racing Commission which, by State Statute, had forty-five days to adopt, modify or reject the Administrative Law judge's decision. Under the rules and statutes, the Executive Director can get at least one extension by request to the Chief Administrative Law judge.

---

[7] A "break" occurs in harness racing when a horse goes off stride and if it is off stride at the finish wire, it is disqualified.

At the time of this appeal, the New Jersey Racing Commission was composed of four Commissioners and its Executive Director, who did not have a vote. Forty-three days after the original Administrative Law judge's decision, and without notice to us, the NJRC met on the matter. Only two Commissioners showed up. Three were required for a quorum. No appearance was afforded to King or his counsel. The next day we received a one paragraph order revising the Administrative Law judge decision and re-imposing the nine-month suspension. The Executive Director could have requested an extension to obtain a quorum but chose not to do so. He made an error.

We appealed the matter to the Superior Court Appellate Division, arguing amongst other points, that in the absence of a quorum the action taken was a legal nullity. The Court accepted that argument and determined that under the "deemed adopted" provision of our state statute, the Administrative Law judge's opinion became the controlling disposition. It ordered the charges against King dismissed.

Naturally, the Executive Director and NJRC couldn't let that stand, as it demonstrated their fault in not requesting an extension when only two commissioners showed up for its "star chamber" hearing. The NJRC petitioned the Supreme Court to review the "uppity nerve" of the Appellate Division and the Court granted review. At oral argument the Court was beside itself to cover for the obvious error.

In the end it simply re-wrote the state statute to give the New Jersey Racing Commission and its Executive Director a pass. They opined that if a public body "tried" within the forty-five-day period to act on a ruling, the "deemed adopted" provision of the state statute would not count. In short, the Supreme Court of New Jersey gave the NJRC and its Executive Director a "mulligan". It cost Jim King his racing career in New Jersey.

The case was remanded back to the New Jersey Racing Commission to take official action. When my client heard this, he accepted the suspension without another appeal and left New Jersey harness racing. He relocated to Delaware and went back to earning a living driving harness horses. During his suspension he simply worked doing other jobs in his beloved occupation.

He has never returned to New Jersey thanks to the NJFR and its Supreme Court.

Jack Moiseyev v. New Jersey Racing Commission, 239 N.J. Super 1 (App. Div., 1989)

In his era, Jack was one of the most successful harness drivers in the United States. He also developed a reputation as "Pecks Bad Boy" with the NJRC racing officials.

During this time period, harness racing was offered in the afternoon at Freehold and at night in the Meadowlands. Race cards generally have between ten and fourteen races a day; it was not unusual for Jack to drive eight starts at Freehold and another seven mounts at the Meadowlands. He earned a substantial living in this fashion.

Yet the racing rules are highly subjective, and the officials pretty much call the shots. If an official is annoyed at a driver or just doesn't like him, he can continue to hand out seven-to-ten-day suspensions for "lack of effort" or "poor judgment" against a driver who'll get no relief on appeal.

In 1987, Jack was on the bad side of Chief Judge P. Virag at Freehold. In one of those afternoon drives, he was cited with a thirty-day suspension because the judge didn't like the way he drove a horse.

The New Jersey legislature established the New Jersey Racing Commission (NJRC)and authorized it to adopt rules to carry out its purpose. It also recognized the United States Trotting Association (USTA) which has its own rules and provided so long as USTA rules were not in conflict with NJRC rules, the USTA rules would supplement the New Jersey ones.

In fact, New Jersey had no rule establishing a penalty for "lack of effort" driving. Meanwhile, the long standing USTA rule provided a ten-day maximum suspension for a "lack of effort" infraction.

The Court issued a lengthy published opinion reducing the suspension from thirty to ten days based on the USTA rule. The Court went out of its way to reject many of my arguments about the amount of control left to the racing officials, taking the road of least resistance to help the driver and limit his penalty.

As in King, I expected a trip to the New Jersey Supreme Court, but was surprised when the NJRC relented, issuing an order for a ten-day suspension. A very small victory for the good guys. Eventually, though, the New Jersey officials wore Jack out, and he left New Jersey to continue a successful career in Canadian harness racing.

For many years, I had been into standardbred racing as a small-time owner and in the 1990s I moved into the thoroughbred racing scene, again as a small-time owner. The impetus for this move came when I met Sydney Underwood, a young lady jockette-trainer who had become a paraplegic as a result of injuries sustained during a race at Atlantic City Race Course on June 19, 1992.

That accident led me on a tour of our courts in South Jersey and into the Third Circuit Court of Appeals in Philadelphia, Pennsylvania.

Underwood v. ACRA, 295 N.J. Super 335 (App. Div., 1996)

and

Underwood v. ACRA, US 3rd Circuit CA, #96-5578, (Decided 3-27-98).

Ms. Underwood was the jockey on a thoroughbred horse one evening at Atlantic City Race Course. As the field of horses came out of the back stretch into the clubhouse turn, her horse dug in its front feet and unseated her. She was thrown like a rag doll over the adjacent rail causing her to fracture her spine and lose all feeling below her mid-back.

I was retained to try and put her life back together, at least to the extent legal claims could produce some economic support for that young lady with a broken body.

We had a worker's compensation claim, a suit for damages in the Superior Court and a claim against the Atlantic City Racing Association (ACRA) and the Jockey's Guild, since they had failed to offer or get the plaintiff onto the roster for the Catastrophic Injury Policy. This was supposed to be available for precisely these situations. Under New Jersey Workers Compensation law, Underwood was eligible to receive payment of reasonable and necessary medical, temporary disability payments, and permanent disability payments over her lifetime. This was due from her employer's worker's compensation carrier, her employer being the trainer of the fallen horse. In addition, if she could prove fault on the part of a third party, she could receive damages, which could be substantial. This would require a jury trial.

If successful, the worker's compensation carrier was protected by a statutory lien and could receive back approximately two-thirds of the money it had paid to the injured worker (or jockey). Future payments would also be reduced.

Here, that would be a substantial amount, as the worker's comp carrier had acted in good faith and provided Underwood with the best care available at a Philadelphia medical center.

The claim for damages in Superior Court, Camden County was fraught with difficulty. We had obtained and reviewed the videotape of the race. It showed that a few feet from the side railing on the racetrack was a shadow of the rail, running in a straight thick line into the turn, then moving out as the horses went into the turn. Plaintiff had told us her horse would not step on or cross that shadow on the straightaway before the turn. As the horse went into the turn it was squeezed by outside horses and had to step on the shadow. When it did, it suddenly dug in two front feet causing it to flip over and the plaintiff to be thrown over the rail. We had a well-respected trainer review the tape and he agreed it appeared the shadow caused the horse to panic.

We also retained a civil engineer who reviewed the plans of Calvi Electric, the electric company that installed the lighting, and the national standards for such installations. He concluded the electrical contractor had negligently aimed the high intensity bulbs, needlessly creating the shadow on the track. There were many known instances of racehorses reacting adversely to shadows on the track and not creating them was a national standard.

While confident we could make out a prima facie case and have a jury decide the matter, I was concerned with whether we could expect a jury to buy into our theory of liability. We also faced a problem with what standard the trial judge would require us to prove in order to succeed. Did we have to prove simple negligence or that Atlantic City and/or Calvi Electric was guilty of "reckless conduct"?

That was a big issue. Our courts had held in informal sports events that if one participant injured another, the injured party could only collect damages if they proved the other party's conduct had been reckless. Simple negligence was not sufficient. While we could differentiate this incident from a pick-up sports case, the defendants were arguing a New York court had thrown out a jockey's case for damages based on the condition of the track. I thought I could distinguish that case from ours, but it wasn't clear cut.

The defendants filed motions for summary judgment on these issues a few months before our trial date. The Camden County Assignment judge had heard our case and fortunately ruled (1) we only had to prove simple negligence; and (2) the New York case was significantly different from our claim so as to be of no moment. I believed I'd been successful in creating a jury question. I know the ruling concerned the two defendants.

We appeared on a Monday morning for trial and were assigned to a gruff senior judge who would try the case with a jury. The defendants had brought an insurance adjuster from Boston to sit in and perhaps settle the case. I had contacted the representative of the worker's compensation carrier and was hopeful that with some assistance from the trial judge, we could work out a settlement.

On arrival at the judge's chambers, his clerk ushered the three attorneys into his office. We discussed the case informally for a few moments and he asked to see the moving papers from the recently decided summary judgment motion and excused us. He was not remotely interested in discussing a possible settlement or in having the defendants' insurance representative partake in any discussions. About thirty minutes later he emerged and without allowing any argument simply dismissed our case for reasons directly contrary to the Assignment judge's findings.

This was done without the defense even asking for a dismissal. We were all shocked by the sudden ending of the case without notice, without argument and without my client present.

A few minutes later my client appeared in her wheelchair. I had to take her into a small room and try to explain to her what had just happened. As I learned, people who have suffered extremely severe trauma often suffer other forms of emotional overlay like anxiety or depression. She wheeled herself out of our meeting room, crying out that she'd had enough and was going to end it all. Over the next several hours, I repeatedly reached out to her psychologist and made sure he remained in contact with her to make sure she didn't end it all.

Her suit, filed in 1992, had been dismissed early in 1996. I filed an appeal from this outrageous action of the old trial judge, a man who didn't give a wit about simple fairness or the Court Rules.

A second suit she had filed in 1995 was also dismissed by a federal judge in September 1996 for violating the New Jersey "entire controversy" rule. In her federal action she had sued the ACRA, as well as the insurance companies that had issued "Jockey Catastrophic Injury" policies and the "Jockey Guild." Underwood's claim here was that the Jockey Guild, in league with ACRA, discriminated against non-guild members by not offering the Catastrophic Injury coverage to them.

Under such a policy, without proof of fault she would have been entitled to an award of $800,000 for her injuries with none of that award subject to a Worker' Compensation lien. I also appealed that dismissal.

A paraplegic person had been treated to outrageous dismissals by two trial courts, one in Superior Court of New Jersey, one in Federal Court in New Jersey. It was and is clear to me their dismissals are compelling evidence that many trial division judges are unfit, unable and/or simply too lazy to dispense justice fairly or evenly. Ms. Underwood's claims were unique and unusual. In each case her lawyer was not a regular in that venue. Each court construed everything against the plaintiff as if her claim was a bother to submit for proper trial adjudication.

The first appeal for the injury claim resulted in a reversal and was remanded for jury trial. The opinion is found at 295 N.J. Super 335 (1996).

In that opinion, while the Court did not call out the trial judge for his misconduct, it did criticize his actions. Further, it made it clear how the case would be treated going forward.

The Federal Appeal also was successful and resulted in a March 1998 opinion sending the case back to trial. In an eighteen-page opinion, Judge Stapleton made short work of the "entire controversy" argument, concluding that the trial court was just plain wrong in its application of that New Jersey concept.

What was lost in all this are two key points. First, litigation exacts a heavy emotional toll on severely injured individuals. Both of Underwood's claims had legitimate factual bases and both were extremely important to her economic existence. Yet, neither trial court had the remotest interest or concern in her well-being. They took the shortest route to rid themselves of the burden of addressing the merits of the claims and were quick to dispense injustice. Neither judge was openly criticized for their inappropriate behaviors and were permitted to move on to their next case ... and perhaps next victim(s).

Second, these cases place a heavy burden on counsel. I took on a case with three angles: (1) A worker's compensation case, where my fee would be 20°/o of the permanent award up to approximately $20,000; (2) A personal injury case entirely contingent on a successful outcome, with nothing extra for a successful appeal; and finally (3) a case brought almost gratis, since the paraplegic plaintiff had no ability to pay. Meanwhile, I had to advance all the costs for experts and trial preparation.

In the end, both cases were settled for a lot less than was just, as the plaintiff was emotionally drained and scarred. By the time each trial was scheduled, Underwood couldn't afford to risk any more uncertainty in a system that had proved its injustice. She had to take the money.

The search for justice is highly uncertain and almost shockingly serendipitous. Most attorneys prefer to put their business sense ahead of their sense of and search for justice.

For me, this has always presented a great moral dilemma, a concept that in all my years I've never been able to set aside. I call it "playing sandbox" and believing that I can use my training, experience and acumen to beguile some justice out of a heartless and broken system.

OTHER END-OF-CENTURY CASES

Waters Edge v. Coyle at al A-151-96T3

The beginning of 1998 produced the Underwood decision from the Third Circuit regarding the "entire controversy" doctrine and another from the Appellate Division in New Jersey, Waters Edge v. Coyle. This opinion was the tip of the iceberg in a dispute between my client E.S., his lender bank, his own civil engineer, the Borough of Keyport and its civil engineer S.D. It took almost seven years to complete and resulted in a high six-figure settlement for my client.

Along the way, another trial judge misapplied justice, causing unnecessary waste of time, expense and anxiety for the claimant. The "entire controversy" doctrine is a judicial-made concept created to stop unfair fragmentation of litigation. Often, in its administration, it causes more trouble than it saves.

In E.S.'s case, after the plaintiffs had lost most of their motions for summary judgment and after plaintiff had lost his investment, the trial judge considered a claim that defendants had known about in excess of three years, and dismissed the case invoking the "entire controversy" doctrine.

Years before, the plaintiff had been served for foreclosure and damages by the bank that had underwritten his building project in Keyport. He consented to the foreclosure and eventually settled the damage claim and dismissed his counterclaim. He had already filed his claim against the Borough of Keyport, its engineer and his former engineer for damages.

During the discovery phase, he had told the defendants about the bank case and its settlement. Three years later, defendants filed a motion for summary judgment based on his failure to join the bank case with the damage claim against the defendants. The trial judge, who had already ruled that plaintiff had sufficient facts to present his case to a jury, opted to throw out plaintiff's case.

On appeal, the Appellate Division made short work of the dismissal and reversed the trial judge. That Court saw the behavior of the defendants and the trial court and sent the case back–for jury trial. That resulted in a reasonable settlement of a difficult situation.

The point of its inclusion here is to show how a trial court decided to clear its calendar by abolishing the plaintiff's case, which was different and difficult for the judge to try. The Court took the shortest route to avoid thinking and dealing with a problem case. No real consideration was given to the feelings of the plaintiff, or even the search for justice. This is the same guy who later trifled with my legal fee.

CDS Recoveries v. Peter DeLamos, A-3310-01T2

This case straddled the end of the 20th Century.

I do not want to condemn all trial judges. There are some outstanding ones. The case of Peter Delamos, in his dispute with CDS Recoveries, LLC illustrates the work of the Honorable Robert Coogan, an exceptionally competent trial judge who consistently searched for justice and tried to do the correct thing with each case. Judge Coogan, now retired, was also instrumental in changing the history and maps of Howell Township, New Jersey in a case found in the third section of this book.

In the CDS Recoveries case, the matter began with an alleged simple guarantee of a commercial loan and a separate mortgage by my client Peter Delamos. The bank issuing the loan went under and was taken over by the FDIC. The matter started in 1989 and finally concluded with Judge Coogan's decision in late 2003.

The FDIC eventually foreclosed the mortgage on the Rumson, New Jersey property Delamos posted as security, but that was not the end of the matter.

Instead, the FDIC sold the note to CDS Recoveries. They, in turn, sued Delamos for the difference between the amount due and the credit from the foreclosure: a deficiency suit. The matter became so complicated it ultimately required two bench trials with an Appellate Division decision in between.

The first bench trial was presided over by Judge P. McGann, since retired and passed on. As a trial judge he always tried to do the correct thing but there were times when his personality got in the way. Here, his instinct was that the FDIC and CDS were not entitled to any more money from Mr. Delamos.

Judge McGann led us on a legal odyssey only concluding well into the 21st century. He had handled the foreclosure action in the Chancery Division which ended with a consent for foreclosure accompanied with a stipulation of dismissal, both with prejudice and internally without prejudice prepared by the lawyer preceding me on the case. At the bench trial of the deficiency claim by CDS he focused on that point and used it as the basis in ruling against CDS and in favor of Delamos, resisting my own efforts to expand the basis of the decision.

As a result of one stubborn trial judge, CDS successfully appealed the case and secured a retrial. This stubbornness affected yet another case discussed later, Fink v. Thompson.

In its opinion, the Appellate Division was constrained to reverse the trial court yet co-opted our argument that "...whatever rights the FDIC had on its deficiency claim were resolved when Delamos agreed to pay the additional amount on the foreclosure sale."

Fortunately, on the remand, Judge McGann had fully retired and the case went to Judge Coogan for disposition. This judge had the appropriate personality and patience to serve as a trial judge. We retried the case and this time the judge latched onto the significant point, quoted above, following the same instinct of Judge McGann but not fumbling the logic. Judge Coogan ruled for my client, ending his nightmare.

It turned out that prior to the sheriff's sale in foreclosure, Delamos had found a buyer willing to pay $30,000 more for the property than the FDIC appraisal. The foreclosure sale was cancelled, Delamos paid the extra money and a third party walked away with the piece of property. This led Judge Coogan to correctly conclude any deficiency had been waived and Delamos was exonerated from further liability.

State v. Miller, 220 N.J. Super 106 (App. Div., 1985)

This reported case arose out of a driving while intoxicated charge which, coupled with another case, altered how DWI cases would be handled in New Jersey. The timing on the publication of the Appellate Division opinion also revealed how New Jersey decisional law is managed by a phantom hand which should be examined and subjected to public scrutiny: The Committee on Opinions. The Committee settles which formal trial and Appellate opinions are published and may be cited as authority by other courts. They are precedential.

In the recent past, New Jersey's policy regarding driving and drinking has become severe. Penalties for driving while intoxicated have been elevated to the point of near absurdity.

Under the old law, all motorists were deemed to have consented to take a breath test by mere operation of their vehicle. Refusal to take the test, resulted in a separate charge and penalty in addition to the DWI charge. In the early 1980s, elected officials decided to toughen the laws against drunk drivers. First, the legislature reduced the presumptive reading for a DWI conviction from a .15% Blood Alcohol Content (BAC) to a .10% BAC. They then took the more radical step of declaring that if the reading at time of operation was a .10% BAC, the defendant was guilty. In effect this delegated the question of guilt or innocence to a machine, under extremely lax rules. The reading from the machine is based on the reading by an officer done without any permanent record of what the machine is *actually* registering. The subject is told to blow into a tube. The machine then analyzes the sample and a needle on a graph moves to a certain fixed point. The officer looks at what it registers and then marks it down. Usually, two tests are given. Realistically, the officer can write down whatever he wants and there is no residual proof of what the machine actually registered.

Notwithstanding this lack of objective control, New Jersey decreed if your BAC. was .10% at the time of operation, you are guilty of DWI. For a first offense you face a six-month suspension of driving privileges, a fine of $250 and a substantial surcharge on your liability insurance–$3,000 at last amendment, plus certain other penalties.

For second and third offenses the penalties are more severe. Curiously, the legislature failed to graduate the seriousness of the offense by whether the conviction is related to a simple stop and arrest, an accident, or an incident involving personal injury to a second party. (These were the penalties when the case was heard.)

Enter, Mr. R. Miller. One evening he was attending a business dinner meeting at a hotel in Somerset County. Sometime after midnight, he set off for his house taking I-287, a superhighway in northwestern New Jersey. He was set upon by two New Jersey State Police officers in a patrol car. It had been a rather uneventful night for these fellows, and they noticed Mr. Miller's car allegedly moving from lane to lane on the Interstate.

The driver of the troop car activated the dome lights and pulled Miller over. He was asked to produce and did produce his driving credentials. The officers, one on each side of his vehicle shining very strong lights directly at him, asked him if he had been drinking. He responded in the affirmative. He was then asked to exit his vehicle and do some field balance tests. Satisfied they had a candidate for a DWI charge, the officers arrested and cuffed

Miller, placed him in the troop car and took him to headquarters for more formal testing, including a couple of breathalyzer tests.

At headquarters, he was asked to perform a series of balance tests and a verbal acuity test. The official policy of the State Police was to not videotape these tests. Many local police departments require use of video, which can be reviewed by the judge and serve as an objective and valuable tool because it records a defendant's condition. Whether for economy or other reasons, the State Police prefer to leave DWI investigations without anything but the officer's subjective opinions.

In any event, Mr. Miller thought he did well on his clinical testing. He was then asked to take the two breath tests. Not feeling drunk, he agreed. The officer recorded readings of .11 and .12% BAC. Miller was then charged with DWI. Our firm was retained to defend the charge.

It is a scientific fact that the BAC level changes relatively rapidly. First, after one drinks a beverage, it may take up to forty minutes before the alcohol is detectable in the lung air sample used for the test. The body will burn off a given amount of alcohol once absorbed into the blood, at a predetermined rate. Based on this natural process, if you have the BAC reading at the time of testing, it is possible to extrapolate the reading at the time of operation. Since the tests may be administered more than one hour after operation, the differences can be appreciable.

Depending on the two readings, it was possible to produce expert testimony who could opine the reading at the time of operation was below 10% -BAC. Since the language of the statute established this standard and specifically used the words "time of operation", that defense was logically correct.

Our expert reviewed the State Police reports and the defendant's factual statement. He opined it was a very close case with Miller's BAC at the time of operation: .09 to .095. The time of Miller's last drink to the time he drove became an important factor.

For our firm, former assistant prosecutor Charles Uliano tried the case in Municipal Court. Miller was convicted. The judge felt if the state produced a reading of .10 BAC there was nothing he could do *but* convict.

We took an appeal to the Superior Court, Law Division. Judge Meredith felt there was reasonable doubt on Miller's guilt, but also felt the readings compelled the conviction.

By this time, I was frustrated by the lack of flexibility shown by the judges. They knew the official policy of the state was to be severe against those charged with DWI and were fearful of construing a statute in a manner which made sense but provided a defense in close cases.

Deciding to take one more stab at the issue, we filed an appeal to the Superior Court, Appellate Division. Luckily, we found there are a few members of the judiciary willing to decide cases on the merits and not some broader policy. They concluded the evidence, considered in totality, compelled a reasonable doubt as to the defendant's status at the time the vehicle was operated. The defendant's expert established the probability the reading at time of operation was not up to .10°/o BAC. The Court took the bold step of acquitting him. However, the Court's opinion was not published, considerably narrowing the decision's impact.

Shortly after that decision, another panel of the Appellate Division, without considering the unpublished State v. Miller case, decided it would not permit defendants charged with DWI to introduce evidence extrapolating later readings back to the time of operation, C. F. S. v. Tischio 208 N.J. Super 343 (App. Div., 1986).

The Tischio ruling was patently inconsistent with the statutory language but, the Court was more concerned with the broad social policy against DWI. The Court's myopic approach did not consider the adverse impact on our traditional notions of fairness.

Ultimately, the Tischio decision was reviewed by the New Jersey Supreme Court which joined the social conscious crowd and held that defendants would not have an opportunity to defend themselves. Then and only then the Miller opinion, no longer good law, was published.

My client, Mr. R.E. Miller was the last of the lucky few to have a DWI case decided fairly on the evidence, not on an unelected jurist's notion of what is in the best interest of the public. The loss to our system is far graver than unfair DWI convictions. Our common law is ill-served by judges strapping broad social policy to individual cases. It is so much better served by adhering to a policy of neutrality, deciding each issue on its own merits regardless of outcome.

Looking at the decision dates of State v. Miller and State v. Tischio, one smells a rat. Miller, decided in August of 1985, wasn't published until *after* Tischio–decided six months after Miller–was decided and published. Tischio is found at 208 N.J. Super Miller in volume 220. Miller's certification was denied by the Supreme Court on June 3, 1986. By then, Tischio had been argued before the Supreme Court with a decision coming in November 1986. Approximately a year later, Miller was approved for publication.

Somebody in judicial officialdom managed the development of the law improperly. If State v. Miller had been timely published, when in 1986 the Tischio defendant petitioned the Supreme Court for review, the Court would have had to address Tischio in light of Miller just to clarify the law. Someone did not want that to happen.

Go back to State v. Turcotte to see the work of the Committee on Opinions improperly controlling our *common* law. Perhaps, aptly named.

END OF THE MIDDLE YEARS

During the last decade of the 20th century, I began to focus my efforts on medical malpractice and the ever more substantial injury cases, as represented in N.S. v. R.E., the last matter offered in these "Middle Years."

N.S. v. R.E.

I took over this medical negligence case from a colleague who wasn't comfortable taking it to trial. He originally had sued a radiologist and OB/GYN physician. Prior to my substitution, the case against the radiologist had been dismissed for failure to provide a supporting expert.

We had a jury trial before Judge Florence Peskoe, one of the first female Superior Court judges in the state. Defending the OB/GYN was Richard Amdur, Esq. possibly the finest defense attorney of physicians in the State of New Jersey.

The allegation against Amdur's client was that there had been no timely follow-up by the doctor who'd been sent a radiologist's report on plaintiff's mammogram. That mammogram revealed a lump in plaintiff's right breast. There was a factual dispute between the plaintiff and her physician on what transpired after the report had been received by his office. The physician blamed the patient; the patient claimed the office staff misled her.

During the trial, the Court had not allowed our expert to give his opinion on the defendant's failure to provide the plaintiff reasonable information on the risks revealed in the report, and to adequately warn her. Our expert was not allowed to offer examples of what plaintiff should have been told to adequately warn her.

The jury returned a verdict against the plaintiff, finding no violation of the physician's standard of care. To me, this miscarriage of justice directly resulted from the trial court's interference with the plaintiff's claim by disallowing critical evidence.

The judge had been intimidated by a defense attorney who'd spent months with her trying medical malpractice cases back to back, the result of which was known as "the Amdur rule." This rule allowed the local assignment judge to park Richard Amdur with a single judge for trials back to back to avoid being pulled to other counties to try cases set up by other assignment judges.

Another decent rule, in principle, but in practice, extremely prejudicial to plaintiffs. The judicial system had not stopped to consider the practical impact of how control of the courtroom would be ceded to defense counsel coupled with a specific judge for months on several malpractice cases. On appeal, we argued the limitations imposed by the trial court on our expert improperly intruded on our right to fair trial. The Appellate Division agreed, reversing the verdict and sending the case back for retrial. During the course of the opinion, the court stated this practice, "the Amdur rule," was fraught with problems of administration.

That opinion was issued on December 5, 1994. Ten years later, when I next tried a case against Mr. Amdur, his assignment to a trial judge for back-to-back trials of medical malpractice cases continued unabated. See the discussion in Fink v. Thompson in the third section of this book.

On re-trial, I petitioned a different judge to reinstate the radiologist as a defendant for the retrial. While the appeal was pending, I had had the mammogram read by an expert radiologist who opined the radiologist had misread the film, which had actually showed a cancerous mass and not simply a "fibrocystic cyst."

Reinstating this claim needed a trial judge willing to do the correct thing and not elevate form over substance. That judge, the late James Kennedy, over strong objection, allowed us to add the radiologist back in as a defendant.

That Order opened the doors for a settlement in excess of a million dollars. The radiologist paid his entire policy and Amdur's client contributed a six-figure number. None of this could reverse the ultimate march of the plaintiff's illness, and she passed away from it. However, the settlement helped rebuild a life for her husband and children. Had we gone to the jury, the case might have brought more, but a trial of these difficult and sophisticated cases often make the search for justice cloudy and obscure. Juries do not like finding doctors at fault, especially physicians who make good appearances as witnesses.

The old maxim teaches "a case settled is a case won." The judiciary is mottled with judges who cannot be counted on to be anything other than "myopic" at best. That was the lesson I learned in the 20th century. With the hundreds of judges I appeared before, only Judges Coogan, Kennedy and a few others could be counted on to see things clearly and correctly. The vast majority were lazy, dumb, institutionally protective, discriminatory or emotionally unfit.

The Twenty-First Century: 2000–present

21st Century Lawyer

This portion of my writing begins with cases started and/or resolved during the year 2000 and onward. Over my career, I served as lead counsel in twenty-one cases where the case settled for at least $1 million, and that amount, or more was in controversy. Of those cases, sixteen concluded in this century.

During this period, I started to limit my practice to major cases including those for the Thoroughbred Horsemen's Association, for which I'd become their litigation counsel. I also took on some major cases for a client with an extremely interesting line of work, i.e., viatical settlements, and a client whose case may have directly affected an entire community in Howell Township, New Jersey: Equestra.

Fink v. Thompson

Fink was a medical malpractice case arising out of the death of a young woman who suffered from an extremely rare form of meningitis (listeria). The case went all the way to the Supreme Court which ruled in our favor and sent the case back for trial. Fink v. Thompson 167 N.J. 551 (2001). At trial, we received a favorable verdict and the case ultimately settled for more than $1 million, after the defense appeal was rejected.

In 1995, the New Jersey Legislature adopted a statute requiring plaintiffs wishing to sue certain professionals obtain a document known as an "affidavit of merit." That statute created a cottage industry in and of itself and accounted for significant injustices, great delays and making the preparation and trial of medical malpractice cases extremely expensive. In 2004 the statute was sharpened to make it even more difficult and expensive to sue physicians. It also attempted to further delineate which physicians could find fault with and testify against another physician. It is incompatible with current medical science. Efforts by the court to make the statute rational and workable have been a failure as far as the plaintiffs' bar is concerned.

When our firm got the Fink case, we hired a neurologist, formerly from John Hopkins in Baltimore, Maryland to review the case and provide the required affidavit of merit. The case involved three physicians associated with Riverview Hospital in Red Bank and several from Robert Wood Johnson in New Brunswick. In his affidavit of merit, our neurologist forgot to mention Dr. Richard Stroebel by name. Under the statute, a plaintiff had 120 days after the last answer was filed to submit a proper "affidavit of merit."

Shortly before the 120th day, realizing Dr. Stroebel had not been specifically named, we filed a request to allow the filing of an amended affidavit. The motion judge was the same one who had botched up the first DeLamos trial. He followed the same pattern, denying us the chance to file the amended affidavit and dismissing the case against Dr. Stroebel.

Since we believed this physician was most responsible for our client's death, we filed a motion for leave to appeal to the Appellate Division. They too were unpersuaded that our cause was just and denied our motion. Not willing to take "no" for an answer, we filed a motion for leave for appeal with the New Jersey Supreme Court and were pleasantly surprised when it granted our application.

Our case was joined with several other similar cases and all argued together before the Supreme Court. In multiple opinions, the Court outlined how and when the statute should be applied and when courts should relax the harsh rules the legislature had created. Our case was sent back for trial against Dr. Stroebel as well as the other named defendants.

Back I went to the Freehold Courthouse for trial before Judge A. Lehrer and a jury. At the time, he was sitting as the "Amdur judge," trying Amdur's cases back-to-back notwithstanding the earlier Appellate Division suggestion noted in N.S. v. R.E. in 1994. Judge Lehrer was the strongest personality and most intelligent trial judge I had encountered since Judge Thomas Yaccarino.

Judge Lehrer took charge of a courtroom and left no room for disagreement through advocacy. During the course of this trial, he didn't like the way I was handling my expert witness from Maryland. He invited me into the hallway with one of the many defense counsels and literally threatened me. When I told him to stay out of how I was handling my witness, he threw a tantrum and stormed back into the courtroom, slamming his rulebook down on the bench in front of the jury.

At conclusion of the trial but before the case was sent to the jury for determination, we had to settle how the court would implement the Scaffidi Rule.[8] This rule had changed the regular method of proving causation when (1) dealing with a medical malpractice case; (2) the plaintiff was suffering with a pre-existing condition; and (3) it was alleged the doctor-defendant had committed negligence making matters worse.

However, here the allegation included an emergency room doctor, a primary care doctor, two neurologists, an intensivist and two residents. This created a logical nightmare for explaining to a jury how the Scaffidi Rule applied and what it meant for the ultimate outcome toward the jury's decision.

---

[8] In Scaffidi v. Seiler, 119 N.J. 93 (1990), the NJ Supreme Court relaxed the "but for" standard for cause in medical malpractice cases, holding there was satisfactory causation if a defendant's negligence contributed to a lost chance of improvement or cure. After the verdict, Judge Lehrer agreed with our analysis and entered the correct judgment in favor of the plaintiff against Dr. Stroebel.

Suffice it to say, we disagreed how the jury should be charged. In the end the jury concluded none of the physicians were negligent except Dr. Richard Stroebel, who was found liable. We then had to straighten out the amount of verdict needing reduction by Scaffidi. Judge Lehrer finally agreed.

The Appellate Division affirmed our verdict and the widower received his money.

It took eight years to conclude the case. We had to fight a war within the New Jersey judicial system to secure justice for the plaintiff. In the end, it was like Ahn v. Kim and Herman v. Sunshine Chemical.

Our Court system simply demands too much to conclude a bona fide claim. It takes all you have, plus some extra and some luck to carry that baton over the finish line.

Five years after the verdict I ran into one of the jurors. She told me she and the rest of the jury found the trial fascinating, another reminder why I keep finding the battles worthwhile.

L. W. v. Delaware Park

In this racetrack accident, the rider suffered severe injuries; not as terrible as in Underwood but still life altering.

On a sunny morning in November 1999 my client L. W. was riding in a practice race with some other horses at Delaware Park. When horses run a practice race, they use the inside of the oval. Horses merely working out run on the outside portion of the track, traveling in the opposite direction.

The practice race began, as three horses sprung from the gate racing all out down along the rail. As they came around the clubhouse turn, a riderless horse was running on the rail in the wrong direction and caused a tremendous collision which lead to the death of two of the animals and severe injuries to the riders.

I was retained to represent L. W. and make a claim against the track and the trainer of the riderless horse. As L.W. was a New Jersey resident, I filed my suit in Federal Court in New Jersey. At first, both defendants claimed they were uninsured for the accident. The other injured riders were all from Delaware and their attorneys initially held up filing actions, concerned with the alleged uninsured status of the putative defendants.

Consequently, my client was the only defendant rider named in a separate suit in Delaware brought by the track against its carrier over the question of coverage. There was an insurance contract for primary coverage of $1 million with a $10 million umbrella issued by Twin Cities Insurance Company.

It was a refreshing exercise to see how intelligently the Delaware Courts and litigants operated. Ultimately, the Delaware Chancery Division ruled that the policies provided coverage based on its construction of policy language which included "practicing for a sports contest." Delaware Racing Association v. Twin City Fire Insurance Company, 2003 W.L. 1605764. We then settled our Federal suit in New Jersey for $1.25 million.

The uninsured trainer also contributed a modest amount and the L. W. case was fully settled. I included this case to compliment the court system as well as the carrier and defendant track litigants for dealing with it in such a positive fashion.

This is in sharp contrast with many New Jersey jurist attitudes where plaintiffs are often considered low lifeforms and the bringing of complicated or unconventional claims is frowned upon.

By the way, I've since learned that New York jurisprudence suffers the same malady as New Jersey's. Delaware was a wonderful and refreshing interlude.

Gonzalez v. Komatsu Forklift USA, 184 N.J. 415 (2005).

Komatsu is another example of this New Jersey contrast. The plaintiff suffered severe injuries when a forklift he was operating ran over him. Another law firm filed a suit against the manufacturer of the lift under the New Jersey Products Liability Act. That suit was dismissed when the trial court concluded the plaintiff's claim was pre-empted by the Federal Occupational Safety and Health Act (OSHA).

That Act had delegated to a private body, the American National Standards Institute (ANSI), the responsibility of establishing regulations and standards covering certain types of equipment. ANSI is made up of manufacturers of these type of products, hardly an unbiased group. They had issued regulations with which the forklift in question was in compliance.

An appeal to the Appellate Division resulted in a split decision, the majority upholding the dismissal, one judge filing a rare dissent, 371 N.J. Super 249. The dissent gave us a right of appeal to the Supreme Court.

With the Chief Justice dissenting, the majority upheld the dismissal of the plaintiff's case, leaving him with an inadequate worker's compensation remedy for his life-altering injuries. Those injuries, and that human loss, is the saddest part of what we do. Very often the jurists deciding these issues seem to forget the consequences of their actions.

From a purely legal perspective, the sad part was how the Court stretched U.S. Supreme Court authority to bar the plaintiff's claim. In his sharp, intelligent dissent, Chief Justice Zazzali stated:

"Here, the Court should not affirm the Appellate Division's finding of preemption for three reasons. First, by including a broad 'savings clause, Congress intended any implied preemption of state tort claims by the Act, to be extremely narrow. Second, state products liability law is generally applicable to all manufacturers and does not regulate employers and employees specifically. Third, imposing tort liability on a forklift manufacture for defective design does not divest forklift users of their discretion to implement safety precautions, but rather encourages the exercise of that discretion with due care."

The majority found an implied preemption to bar the claim, citing a case where a state had passed a law directly opposite what a Federal Regulation had provided for, Gade v. National Wasters Manufacturers Association, 505 U.S. 88 (1992).

The ANSI regulation used in Komatsu left the manufacturer a safety choice. It was that exercise of discretion that the majority illogically immunized. Zazzali called a spade a spade when he concluded:

"To be sure, the Appellate Division sets forth a creative argument, which the majority adopts, in favor of preemption on these facts. The dilemma is that, however appealing its reasoning may seem, the Court's thesis rests on distinguishable precedent, runs counter to the plain language of the Act, and conflicts with Congress's intent to allow common law actions to proceed except in the clearest cases."

Our highest Court had stretched and misinterpreted Federal precedent and ruled contrary to the Federal law, including Congressional intent. To achieve this unjust result, it did a lot of inferring, revealing the Court to be almost bizarrely result-oriented. Our Bar should demand more intellectual honesty from our Bench and call out its anti-plaintiff bias. J'ai accuse!

Another recent case of this bias is Nicholas v. Mynster, 213 N.J. 463 (2013), where the court, contrary to its own precedent in Fink v. Thompson, dismissed plaintiff's case with prejudice, concluding plaintiff had the wrong specialist on his affidavit of merit. No allowance was made for plaintiff's good faith effort at compliance, and the court wouldn't consider the amicus request challenging the law.

Something is very wrong with this picture, though I reiterate: it is not always so troubling. Not all members of the Bench subscribe to this anti-plaintiff bias. The next two trial court decisions demonstrate how the courts can be evenhanded and rational.

Sherman v. Howell Township
and
Relli v. Liberty Mutual

Both cases occurred a few years after the turn of the century. The product of Sherman v. Howell Township can be seen when driving east on old Route 33 between Freehold and Wall Township.

You will pass an active adult community known as "Equestra." This development was the product of an effort by my clients, Tony and Terry, who saw an unused piece of real estate and envisioned building a high-end adult community which was much needed in Monmouth County. They put together two unused adjacent parcels of real estate, obtained Planning Board approval, and contracted to convey the parcel to a famous mass builder, Centex Homes.

Suddenly, their plan was confronted with a recalcitrant seller of one of the parcels and an ugly political problem when the local government leadership changed from Democratic to Republican.

We initiated a civil suit in Superior Court to compel the recalcitrant seller to honor his contract. Meanwhile, the Republican leaders tried to revoke planning approval for the entire project.

It turned out that Tony had made a large donation to the Monmouth County Democratic organization. Shortly after that, the Mayor of Howell Township had received a political job. The Republican County Prosecutor seized records from the Democratic organization and the local planning board. Based on the allegations only, the new local board revoked the prior planning board approval. No criminal charge was ever filed.

We went to court for a second case against Howell Township and its officials. The judges assigned to the two cases both saw through what was happening. In one, the stubborn seller was simply trying to put the squeeze on Tony and Terry.

In the other, one party was trying to punish my clients because of their political affiliation. When these courageous judges made known to the litigants their opinions on the defendant's positions, their claims folded, and I had the distinct pleasure of attending the closing and handing a check for more than $35 million to my clients.

Judges Louis Locascio and Robert Coogan (CDS fame) saw through the efforts to derail the project and ensure justice was done.

During one of the hearings in the case against Howell Township, Judge Coogan commented that in his twenty-some years on the Bench, he had never seen a serious allegation contending a public body had passed a "Bill of Attainder." That rather arcane concept prohibits a legislative body from passing a bill forfeiting a property right or valuable asset without a trial and appears in Article 1, Section 9 of the U.S. Constitution.

We had made that allegation–knowing it was a bit of a stretch–on our motion for summary judgment against Howell Township, claiming its resolution revoking the Planning Board approval was just such an illegal act. We laughed about the claim, counsel and judge alike. Counsel for Howell Township finally saw the light and settled the case, rather than invite Judge Coogan's wrath on its officials. By settling they saved the public my counsel fees.

Every time I drive past "Equestra," I think about the thousands of people whose homes were built because of the courage of Judge Coogan ... and his sense of humor concerning the old bill of attainder ruse.

The Relli case resulted in a trial court decision written by Judge A. Lehrer, Relli v. Liberty Mutual Fire Insurance Company, found at 2004 W.L. 2360040 (N.J. Super., Chan Div.). Another victim of the Committee on Opinions.

Here, the judge was asked to allow an injured plaintiff to reform her insurance policy after an auto accident. We claimed reformation was justified based on the failure of plaintiff's insurance carrier to provide sufficient information in the mandated "Buyers Guide" to enable her to make a knowing and informed decision on whether to choose the cheaper policy with a verbal threshold, or a more comprehensive coverage which had no limitation on the right to sue for damages.

New Jersey had adopted a law limiting lawsuits under a verbal threshold when an insured selected a policy allowing suit only where the plaintiff suffered permanent injury, defined in the law as "when the subject body part had not and would not heal to function normally even after further medical treatment."

The plaintiffs had selected that limited right to sue after reviewing the buyer's guide sent to them by Liberty Mutual. After that provision, but before their auto accident, the Appellate Division in James v. Torres, 354

N.J. Super 386 (App. Div. 2002) had ruled that, to pursue a claim under their selection, the injured party also had to prove the injury had a serious life impact. This requirement was not contained in the buyer's guide and amounted to a judicially ordered additional requirement beyond the legislative definition of permanent injury–another anti-plaintiff biased decision from our courts. See Emmer v. Merin, 233 N.J. Super 568 (App. Div. 1989).

The James case had been highly criticized by many scholars and attorneys, including me. When our clients advised that they would have selected the broader coverage if they had only known of this added requirement, we then instituted a suit to reform their policy so they could maintain their action for damages.

Judge Lehrer conducted a plenary hearing and issued a written opinion, not published, which took the unprecedented step of permitting our client to obtain the right to sue without limitation. The case was appealed to the Appellate Division and after oral argument, settled as if plaintiff did have the unfettered right to sue.

The real culprit was the Appellate Court in the James case which felt it had the right to alter the legislative scheme by implying additional legislative intent of further conditions on the right to sue. Our timid Supreme Court denied certification to review that case.

The trial court, though very familiar with this anti-plaintiff structure, had the intestinal fortitude to do the right thing and do justice for my client. The Committee on Opinions, which only publishes what legal precedent it wants established, did not order the opinion published, even though it was a monumental ruling.

After receipt of a copy of the opinion, the Department of Insurance made sure the buyer's guide included reference to the James Court requirement that the injury be both permanent and have a serious life impact. Two years later, James was finally reversed by a slightly less timid New Jersey Supreme Court in DiProspero v. Penn, 183 N.J. 477 (2005). There, the Court had been forced to review the issue by a rare dissent in the appellate division. In the interim, many plaintiffs with a verbal threshold had suffered dismissal of their cases because of the misguided James decision; a grave injustice.

Both cases are examples of how our trial courts can affect so many lives with their rulings. Here, Judges Coogan, Lehrer and Locascio were more interested in justice than political popularity. There is a wide gap between a Judge simply doing what he or she thinks is correct or doing what he or she thinks is expected.

More Racing Cases

My professional conflict with the NJRC continued into the 21st century. The clearest example of how personal it was (and is) can be found not so cleverly hidden in the opinion of the court in In the Matter of: Consider Distribution of the Casino Simulcasting Special Fund (2005) In The Amount of $1,820,699.42 Pursuant to N.J.S.A. 5:12-205(d), 308 N.J. Super 7 (App. Div., 2008).

The opinion, certainly the longest captioned in my career, overturned NJRC action blocking my speaking at a public hearing of the Commission where I was addressing the distribution of the earnings from Casino Simulcasting. Funds taken out of that endeavor were required to be shared with the tracks and associations connected to racing in New Jersey. The NJRC ran its public session with few rules and not much public input, including disallowing any oral presentation before it voted on distribution. They silenced me from raising any questions at its "public portion" of the meeting.

On the appeal, a panel of our Appellate Division agreed, reversed the order of distribution and remanded the case to the NJRC to comply with the opinion.

That opinion was issued on January 22, 2008. It included the finding that the Commission had violated the Open Public Meetings Act by engaging in private deliberations and then taken a public vote. It now required the NJRC to conduct its deliberations in public.

The court also held that the NJRC violated the Administrative Procedure Act by not adopting formal regulations to carry out its legislatively delegated duties regarding Commission activities, and not complying with administrative due process.

Finally, the court required the NJRC adopt regulations establishing how it would resolve contested matters in an informal manner, consistent with due process.

In less than one year, another panel of our Appellate Division considered itself free to ignore the remand order. The NJRC had attempted to adopt regulations regarding steroid use in horses without acting on the orders continued in the January 8, 2008 published opinion. We took the matter to the Chancery Division and obtained an injunction of the NJRC to stop it from adopting the steroid rules. The NJRC filed a motion for leave to appeal, which was granted. That Appellate Court was more interested in protecting the NJRC than seeing its own published opinion followed and enforced.

On March 31, 2009 a different Appellate Division panel issued an opinion depriving the trial court of jurisdiction and freeing the NJRC to continue its practice of violating the Open Public Meeting Act law and the Administrative Procedure Act. Later that same year, the court backed further away from its own published opinion, allowing the Commission to deliberate adopting steroid regulations in closed session. The two opinions are found at 2009 W.L. 815440 and 2009 W.L. 4547025, both unpublished. The NJRC did not like the published case found at 398 N.J. Super. 7, and found six other judges who were willing to do its bidding rather than enforce and uphold the stated law. It was King v. NJRC, 103 N.J. 412 (1986) all over again. The law was ignored to carry out some judicial policy.

The courts have continued to deflect attempts to provide horsemen real due process where charged with drug associated offenses. The Appellate Division continues to refuse to force the

Executive Director to issue stays of suspension, thereby mooting many substantial, substantive claims.

A classic example is the case of R.C. v. NJRC, 2011 W.L. 2135, decided January 26, 2011. The trainer was stuck with a double suspension. The NJRC first suspended the trainer, and then refused to reissue a license because of the suspensions, but the court would not stay the suspensions. Yet, the same court found merit in the argument that challenged the validity of the testing technique thusly supporting the suspensions in issue, having been put in issue by plaintiff's expert Michael Lindiger.

At a plenary ruling a year after denying interlocutory relief, the Appellate Court remanded the case back for a plenary hearing, dispensing with most of the claims as moot. There was no consistency with the court's logic. No matter that it denied R.C. 's claim for licensure and told us to go exhaust our administrative remedies before the Office of Administrative Law. This, despite a state statute which favored renewal of an occupational license pending review. N.J.S.A. 5:12-205(d).

That opinion further violated the court's own entire controversy rules by creating two separate cases to be considered without giving any interlocutory protection to my client's now-unlicensed status. When the client read this opinion he simply gave up, told me he was accepting the situation and wouldn't permit me to go forward with his case in any form.

Two years later, he got his license again and went back to training. In all, he suffered a four-year license suspension simply because an administrative law judge misapplied the O.A.L. rules by granting a summary disposition in the face of a valid opinion contrary to the opinion of the plaintiff's expert—who was the State's own chemist. The serious questions of testing and whether or not those rules were really 'junk science' were never addressed. This was recognized by the court on its remand, but it remained totally unconcerned with the trainer's license. The Appellate Division had backpedaled from Luchento, Turcotte and Pelling, issued twenty-five years prior. Horsemen could count on our courts' continued lack of concern for their rights and access to justice.

The Crys Dream Fiasco

The Courts' hands-off posture continued, as evidenced by treatment in the Crys Dream matter. This case involved a 3-year old filly trotter which had won several consecutive races, including a major race event in Canada.

The owners were preparing the horse for a try on Hambletonian Day in a race against either male 3-year old trotters or the top 3-year old trotting fillies at the Meadowlands on the first Saturday in August 2011. Participation in these races was extremely valuable.

A day after the big Canadian win, the trainer was notified that the horse had tested positive for a metabolite of Effexor, a human anti-depressant drug. Under Canadian law, the horse was immediately suspended for 90 days; the owners and trainers suffered losses and penalty without proof of fault or complicity and without a hearing.

In New Jersey, the trainer alone is strictly liable if his horse tests positive. Generally, the horse can be suspended for up to seven days while the State Police finish its investigation.

When Crys Dream arrived at the Meadowlands to prepare for either the Hambletonian or Hambletonian Oaks races, the owners were advised by the racing secretary that he would not accept the entry due to the 90-day Canadian suspension which was under appeal in Canada.

We were retained and immediately requested a hearing and stay of suspension from the Executive Director of the NJRC.

What followed was a shocking eye-opener for the naive owners. First, when it appeared the case involved some legal issues of first impression in New Jersey, mostly jurisdictional, the Executive Director required a silly hearing before a Board of Judges.

After the hearing before the judges' panel on deciding any of those issues, the Executive Director waited just long enough to disqualify the horse from its next entry before addressing our stay request. Then, of course, he denied the stay, though the unusual circumstances had raised genuine constitutional issues.

We rushed to file an emergent appeal from the stay denial by the same executive director. A panel of the Superior Court, Appellate division, with the Attorney General opposing our application, denied our request for stay.

On these applications, litigants aren't even given reasons for the action. Instead, we get a checked box. The standard determining the court's intervention is vague and totally at odds with basic fairness. However, since the 1970s the court has glossed over that murky area of procedure with an "X" marked in a box. There is an eerie similarity to an "X" used by an illiterate who cannot sign his name and these distinguished judges using an "X" to deny justice.

With the owners' rights to compete in the 2011 "Grand Circuit" hanging in the balance, we filed an emergent motion with the New Jersey Supreme Court.

Much to our delight-and surprise-the Court granted our motion and directed the NJRC to allow the horse to compete, at least through full administrative adjudication of the legal issues in the case. This was an extremely unusual ruling from our Supreme Court. Alas, it was of no significant import.

After missing two important weeks of racing, Crys Dream was allowed to try to qualify for the big race. On a warm Friday night in July, the horse went out and won her race, ensuring her entry for the Hambletonian Oaks the following Saturday.

Several members of our legal team attended that race and even participated in the picture ceremony after the win. Ultimately, she finished third in the Hambletonian Oaks. Still, the horse earned over $100,000 in the two races.

Meanwhile, the Executive Director continued his campaign against the owners and the horse by impounding the winnings. He carefully crafted his administrative actions to block a single review of the entire case, transferring the appeal of his judges' action to the Office of Administrative Law and separately impounding the purse money.

We asked the NJRC en banc to review that action and it refused, as the matter was already with the O.A.L. We then asked the Federal court to address our legal arguments challenging the Executive Director's impounding the funds. That was the Fall of 2011. The Federal court would not touch the issue either. In February 2014, the Federal court, at the parties request, placed the case on the inactive list until after the opinion from the Appellate Division of September 6, 2014.

Meanwhile, the O.A.L. took jurisdiction of our appeal. After nine months it issued its opinion, concluding New Jersey should not enforce the 90-day horse expulsion. This judge refused to touch the issue of the impounding of the purse money but did hint in a footnote that such action violated the New Jersey Supreme Court Order which had directed the horse be permitted to race.

Under New Jersey law, the O.A.L.'s action needed to be reviewed expeditiously by the NJRC. However, it took that distinguished body five months to issue its opinion setting aside the Administrative Law judge's opinion and directing forfeiture of the earned purse money, even though the purse money issue was not part of that case. The NJRC's decision still ran afoul of the earlier 2008 Appellate Division opinion, which required open deliberation. Again, it deliberated in secrecy and went into its public session with a pre-written opinion before oral argument, which the Executive Director limited to five minutes.

Back we went to the Superior Court, Appellate Division, and after more extensive delays argued the case before a two-judge panel on May 21, 2014. On September 5, 2014 their opinion concluded the NJRC had violated the owners' rights to procedural due process and violated the Administrative Procedure Act with its delay in reaching a final judgment.

Racing jurisprudence in New Jersey is nonexistent. The court's hands-off attitude persists and the NJRC is left to its own maltreatment of its licenses, its own procedures, and the law.

During this legal odyssey, the owning partnership had been dissolved, the horse sold and retired, and the owners left totally frustrated by the Executive Director and NJRC's myopic view of due process. Once again, with limited exception, the courts proved to be nearly irrelevant towards the needs of those they are supposed to serve.

Strangely, the NJRC did not petition the Supreme Court for review of the findings of the Appellate Division which were so highly critical of its actions.

The NJRC finally released the impounded funds to the owners but refused to pay the owners' attorney fees which were in the modest six figures, but more than the winnings. Reluctantly, we reactivated the Federal Civil Rights lawsuit.

The NJRC moved to dismiss the case. The US Magistrate granted most of the motion, leaving us only a minimal area to proceed. We then appealed that decision to a federal judge. After spending hours preparing for oral argument, at our appearance the judge called the parties' counsel in and advised that the NJRC's motion "had some problems." She gave the NJRC until January 8, 2016 to come up with a real offer. On the 8th, the Attorney General advised us the offer was "zero." This position was in the face of two court opinions highly critical of the NJRC's conduct and that of its Executive Director, and a federal judge advising them that there were 'problems with their position.'

Rather than waste more money on Court fees, I submitted the issue to the federal judge "on the papers." That was January 8, 2016. We are in the 5th year of this litigation. It was spawned by the Executive Director's stubborn and arbitrary refusal to let a horse race, refusal to grant a stay, impounding race proceeds, and finally delaying and misleading all connected to the case. He's had an illegal tantrum and our courts are struggling not to offend him, while maybe letting the owners receive a molecule of due process.

It is difficult to imagine the staying power of the owners or any other litigant to have the guts, let alone funds, to believe in anything and rely upon our unreliable court system to mete out justice. "Ulysses" has nothing on these owners.

In August 2017 we received the Federal Judge's opinion leaving the Magistrate's opinion intact. Then the Attorney General filed its appeal to the Third Circuit Court of Appeals.

Finally, after submitting the case for decision in 7-2018, the Appeals Court issued its opinion and agreed with our position. As punishment to the NJRC, the Court awarded us costs. As of this writing we are waiting to see if the NJRC will recognize that it has "problems" with its case.

Ultimately the civil case settled for $22,500–a pittance–because the owners ran out of patience with our court system. I have no adequate words to describe that case.

Four other 21st century cases are instructive of our continuing efforts.

One included a trial, verdict, appeal, and settlement of an unusual situation where the plaintiff walked away with a meaningful settlement and perhaps had the last laugh.

Two others were tragic childbirth cases where the physicians involved simply failed to measure up to the challenges of the difficult circumstances that can develop in pregnancy by applying patience and insight to avoid disaster. The doctors were simply not up to the task. One case ultimately resulted in the death of a seven-year old. In the other, a little boy remains badly disabled but hanging on to life.

Fourth was a tragic accident where I received help from an unexpected source.

These cases all demanded intense focus and brought out my best. And I was helped by members of my firm and some knowledgeable, dedicated experts. These are the types of matters I now handle, and which will likely conclude my legal career.

E.D. v. The Mall

Plaintiff, a plumber by trade, was on a job in a North Jersey strip mall. Two other employees were working with him. While climbing a ladder to enter a crawl space above the ceiling, a portion of it collapsed and the ladder and plaintiff dropped eight feet onto concrete flooring below.

That's when things didn't follow the expected and ordinary course. Instead of reporting the ceiling collapse and his apparent injury to the building owners, his boss continued working him. At the end of the workday plaintiff drove home.

Over the next several months, the plumber developed back complaints and started to see physicians. His condition worsened over the next few years to the point he could no longer work or even stand up straight.

Various medical providers attempted, unsuccessfully, to stem his march toward total disability. By the time the case came up for trial, a local neurologist opined the fall had induced spinal trauma, producing a complete breakdown of his ability to straighten up and walk.

In preparing for trial, we submitted the case for a mock jury trial review. The plaintiff was a terrible witness, and afterward we spent hours schooling him on how to testify. On the eve of trial, I was finally able to find and speak to a co-worker who'd witnessed the fall. He turned out to be a star witness, corroborating the unusual event.

Beginning in law school and throughout practice we are taught how proper trial preparation can make a difference in the result. When the plaintiff got on the stand, he delivered the goods.

Finding an eyewitness, using a practice trial, serious schooling on how to testify, spending considerable time working with an expert and really studying the record; that was our winning recipe. Working together with one of our young associates, we took a highly doubtful case and turned it into a major win.

The judge thought very little of my client or the case when the trial started. However, after the plaintiff testified, the judge called counsel into chambers and urged the defense to come up with a substantial settlement offer. The insurance company for the property owner had evaluated the case as fully defensible and was not prepared to offer any real money.

Thus, the case was submitted to the jury which found the owner liable and awarded the plaintiff $2.5 million dollars. The insurance policy limit was set at $1 million, so we had what is known as a Rova Farms situation.

Rova Farms is a case where the New Jersey Supreme Court set up a standard of care for liability insurers which included a duty to proceed in good faith and, if possible, protect its insureds from situations where a verdict would exceed the policy limits. Here I'd offered to settle the claim well within the million-dollar limit even after the trial judge urged the carrier to offer a substantial sum. The insurer had never offered more than $150,000, thereby exposing its policyholder to the verdict we obtained.

The defendant appealed the verdict and we filed a new suit against the carrier claiming a Rova Farms violation. At argument in the Appellate Division the court made it clear it was concerned with counsel's remarks during summation.

Courts have extraordinary power to set aside a verdict they don't like. In a traditional sense it was hard to like plaintiff's case and the jury verdict was generous. The summation argument started with defense counsel attacking my client as a liar and something akin to a criminal based on his testimony. I attacked what I saw as a false defense and spared no invectives in expressing how the defense's "hired guns" were unworthy of belief.

In view of the court's warnings, I thought it best to work out a settlement above the policy limits but less than the carrier's total exposure. With my client's agreement, we settled both cases for a little less than $1.5 million—almost ten times the defense's final offer.

Approximately one year later I discovered the plaintiff was suffering with an intractable case of M.S., a diagnosis quite different than that attested to by our treating physician. Sometimes, discretion is the better part of valor and stubbornness.

Many years before I had obtained a $65,000 verdict for a lady who fell at the mall. The defendant appealed, and after oral argument had offered to settle for a little more than half that. I'd turned it down. The Appellate Division simply took the verdict away from us, dismissing it. A hard lesson. I wasn't going to make the same mistake again.

That case was followed with three cases settled for amounts between $3.3 and $5 million. They all came with me when I joined the Lomurro law firm in September 2005. One settled just months later. My new associates were immediately happy with their new associate.

S.C. v. Belmar

S.C., a single parent, worked in Belmar, New Jersey on the "head boats"– charter fishing vessels. One evening, back at the docks, her friend was cleaning fish for one of the boat's patrons. When completed, he gave her enough of a tip to buy a "happy meal."

When S.C. challenged the man for being so cheap, he offered to double the tip if she would dive off the dock into the Shark River. She took the challenge and dove into what she thought was several feet of water. The dark water was only eighteen inches deep; that dive off the dock fractured her spine, taking a child's mother from her for the rest of what turned out to be her tragically short life.

I filed a Title 59 claim against the Borough of Belmar which owned the dock, and eventually a suit claiming the defendant had failed to provide a warning of the extremely low water and failed to remind invitees not to dive off the dock into those uninviting waters.

In these cases, it is imperative to obtain the support of a qualified expert and find some supporting standards breached by the defendant.

Over the years I had developed a special relationship with a civil engineer who did most of my forensic engineering work, William Poznak of Knapp Underwood fame. Since he was a specialist in construction, concrete, and slip and fall incidents, I didn't consult him in this case, retaining instead the services of a sea captain who had been around boats and docks most of his life. He had written a report, not too persuasive, that the defendant had failed to provide adequate warning, but hadn't supported his opinion with any objective standards. The defendant provided a few defense reports which seemed to persuasively argue the accident was primarily the plaintiff's own fault. They referenced Red Cross standards which appeared to put the onus on our client.

As a result, the case looked very tough and the defense advised it would never offer anything like a reasonable settlement. They filed a motion for summary judgment about two weeks before I left my own firm to join the Lomurro firm.

At my new firm, I received some serious help from Tom Comer and other firm members. We provided a reasonable case to prevent summary judgment, which luckily was heard by Judge Louis Locascio, a jurist I mentioned earlier as one of the few, rational ones in my experience.

The case was argued on a Friday, and in a coincidence of enormous magnitude, my engineering friend happened to be in the court room during oral argument. Tom Comer argued our case and convinced the judge to deny motion for summary judgement and let the case go forward to a jury trial.

The following Monday, Poznak called and excoriated me for not retaining him. It turned out his expertise included dock-related accidents. He asked me to provide him with the defense expert reports and invited me to his office the following Saturday.

Naturally, I showed up at his office with hat in hand. He told me the defense expert had tried to pull a fast one in citing the Red Cross's standard. What the defense expert failed to mention was the prior section of the same Red Cross manual clearly placed a burden on the dock owner to place warning signs on the dock regarding low water and "no diving signs" to ensure the safety for those using the dock.

My expert friend prepared a thorough report and supplemented our case with this document which clearly established the Borough of Belmar's fault. Though the plaintiff's claim would be reduced by some comparative negligence, it was clear we had a strong breach of written standards by the defendant.

Two weeks later, I received a call from my adversary advising they wished to go to mediation to try and settle the case. A retired judge handled the mediation and my partner and I succeeded in getting a measure of financial security for our client and her family by securing a $3.3 million settlement. We structured a good portion of that, increasing the settlement to close to $5 million.

S.C. was confined to a wheelchair for the rest of her life. That life did not last long, and her daughter was raised by the two grandmothers. The money we obtained has gone a long way to providing a measure of financial security for her family.

E.D. was an ode to how hard work and preparation pay off. S.C. showed how sometimes you need more to complete a complex puzzle. That "more" can be simply some good luck or other subtle intervention. In that case, it was an expert engineer serendipitously sitting in a courtroom.

The Dr. H. Matter

It started with a lovely young couple who needed some help achieving fertility. The defendant was a well-respected neo-natal high-risk specialist who turned out to be a corrupt charlatan who should have had his medical license pulled. In-vitro fertilization comes with a risk of multiple fertilizations. When this occurs, it increases the odds the woman will have difficulty reaching term with any of the fetuses. She then faces the stress of discontinuing some of the fetuses, with a process called "reduction".

A cottage industry has emerged in the pregnancy field with specialists who, in cases of multiple fertilizations, perform a voluntary reduction of the live fetuses by injecting heart-stopping medication into the fetus in situ. The mother is then left with one or two normal fetuses for delivery.

Here the plaintiff used in vitro and was presented with four fetuses. The defendant physician, Dr. H., advised the plaintiff her uterus would never carry all four lives to term, and strongly recommended a reduction from four to two. The procedure was carried out in the doctor's office. He selected two to receive the heart-stopping injection directly through the fetal sack. The mother returned one week after the procedure, and strangely the doctor was able to detect 3 heart beats. As a result, he insisted on a second procedure to try to eliminate one of these living fetuses.

He carried out a second procedure, and plaintiff was left with two live fetuses. At the period between 18 and 20 weeks, Dr. H.

carried out a very specific, sophisticated ultrasound to examine the two live fetuses. On this level two ultrasound, he discovered one of the fetuses had an apparent anomaly in its skull. The defendant told the plaintiff he had detected a slight problem, much like water on the brain, and advised plaintiff to ride it out to term. Nothing else was done to determine what the neurologic problem was, and no serious thought was given to terminate the pregnancy.

A few months later, plaintiff gave birth to two live fetuses. One was normal and vital. The other, "Ryan", suffered a seizure shortly after birth. The child was heavily sedated, and an MRI of the brain obtained. The MRI disclosed that more than 50% of Ryan's brain was missing. The space where brain matter should have been was filled with spinal fluid. Ryan was condemned to a limited life with grave, extremely challenging disabilities.

Ryan was referred to the Children's Hospital in Philadelphia and came under the care of a geneticist who had a colleague at the University of Chicago Medical Center, William Dobyns. These physicians, at the top of their profession, concluded that during the attempted and failed reduction, Dr. H. had injected the potassium chloride into Ryan's brain instead of his chest. When repeating the procedure, he had injected one of the other two normal fetuses, destroying one and leaving Ryan with a severely injured brain. When the level two ultrasound was done at the 18th week of gestation, the anomaly depicted was Ryan's brain injury.

With that information in hand, Ryan's parents contacted me to determine if a viable claim of professional negligence could be successfully prosecuted against Dr. H.

To answer that question, I needed an opinion from a physician in the same field as plaintiff's high-risk doctor; an expert opinion that the cause of Ryan's disability came from the attempted reduction, not some other source. That search led me to Houston, Texas and Chicago, and to a couple of brilliant physicians.

The standard of care expert was Dr. Robert J. Carpenter of Houston, Texas. He was highly critical of Dr. H., especially for his failure to offer any diagnostic studies after discovery of the anomaly on the ultrasound. Carpenter reasoned that after the incident with the failed reduction, Dr. H. had a duty to try to find out more about the anomaly since, without more information, the doctor was risking everything that it was only some limited hydrostatic problem. As it turned out, the fetus had been grievously injured intracranially.

Dr. William Dobyns of the University of Chicago Medical School went to work to prove a link between the attempted reduction and the loss of brain matter and development of all lobes in Ryan's brain.

The study was incredibly advanced. At first, Dr. Dobyns was reluctant to make the connection between injection and injury because he could not account for Ryan's web foot. This was a very strange anomaly. In a feat of stupendous luck, we found an article from France, written in French, that had reached an unusual conclusion for newborns who presented with the same web foot anomaly.

At about 11-13 weeks of gestation, pregnant women often voluntarily undergo a procedure called amniocentesis. The article we found concluded that the needle penetration of the fetal sack at this point in pregnancy could cause the web foot anomaly. It was a risk of the procedure.

Dr. H. had done the attempted reduction during the eleventh week of plaintiff's pregnancy and penetrated Ryan's fetal sack with the needle. When Dr. Dobyns considered this article, he dropped his concerns and supported our case, 100%.

Dr. Dobyns's reports and testimony were so compelling that, after his second deposition in Chicago, the defense decided to settle the case.

We'd also uncovered the fact Dr. H. had been involved in a dozen malpractice claims, had made misstatements on his application for privileges, had been suspended from practice for drug abuse, had been found guilty of sharp billing practices and was less than a good employer toward his staff.

With the combination of Dr. Dobyns's astute deposition testimony and the damning information we'd discovered about the defendant, the defense decided to settle the case.

The defense had claimed it had only $2 million available in coverage. However, when it sent its representatives to mediation at our office, they concluded there was $4 million in coverage, and we convinced the carrier to pay $3.8 million to settle the claim.

Despite the unbelievable amount of work we had done, we needed to get court approval of our legal fee. The client agreed with the amount we requested, but Judge Sullivan disallowed $18,000 of our request. This was for no reason other than judicial jealousy and his wish to demonstrate arbitrary power. This from a judge I had previously helped get reappointed a few years before.

Talk about taking some of the icing off the cake!

Our clients were shocked by his action. I was not. It was just that sort of judicial action that motivated me to write this book. We had taken a case of tough liability, difficult causal relationship, and a dispute on coverage and obtained a settlement of 95% of available funds for a plaintiff who was unwilling to go through with a public trial.

The client had willingly approved our fee request, but a judge who had nothing to do with the case placed his hand in our pockets and removed $18,000.

He did it because he could do it. No appeal was taken since trial courts are vested with something called "discretion."

Our plaintiffs had their loving but disabled son for seven years before he was taken from them, leaving them only with an emotional hole few of us, fortunately, ever have to endure. The money had helped make those seven years easier. But nothing, really, would ever make up for their loss.

M.F. v. MMC

Each Christmas I receive a card from M.F.'s family reminding me how well their son is, no thanks to the staff at a major Monmouth County hospital.

Young Michael is suffering the lifetime effects of oxygen deprivation suffered during a flawed labor and delivery that could and should have been avoided. This foul up was courtesy of (1) a nurse who didn't want to sound the alarm of an impending crisis; to bother (2) an absentee physician who didn't want to disturb his office hours; and (3) an experienced resident who didn't "pull the baby," simply passing the problem to the private physician who was seemingly always just; (4) "on the way in" to deal with a life-altering emergency.

The hospital had an ambiguous policy on dealing with a private patient of a physician who had admitted the mother for birth of her child and left the scene. The patient was left totally dependent on staff nurses and residents to address any emergency development after the private physician had medicated the patient to induce labor.

The newborn baby and its parents were victimized, their future lives marked forever with debility, pain and dysfunction. No amount of money could ever make things right. Our system can only measure fault-causing injury in terms of money. Here, with the help of a talented mediator, the case was settled for five million dollars. Looking critically at the misconduct producing this tragedy one sees failure in the structured components of what is designed to be an extremely safe medical facility.

It started without incident: a private physician decides to admit his patient into the labor and delivery department of a teaching hospital. The nurses are well-trained, and residents address ordinary labor events. The department is equipped with state-of-the-art devices installed for the safety and well-being of mother and fetus.

The private physician starts a morning initiation of induced labor for a patient who was at term plus. He then leaves the hospital with instructions to call him if there are any problems.

Problem occurs, but the nursing staff fails to alert the physician. The heart monitor for the baby starts to warn that the baby is beginning to have trouble. The physician, who has an office full of patients, does not drop everything and come in.

Instead, a highly qualified resident, who'd been a practicing OB/GYN physician in India, sees the patient. Rather than discuss the case with the absent physician, who is available for consultation, he opts to simply reposition the mother, causing a short-term improvement to the baby's heart strip. He leaves, kicking the can down the road. But it isn't a can. It's a live baby, soon to go into full distress.

The disaster comes, the baby suffering oxygen deficit and permanent brain damage before he can be taken from his mother by caesarian section.

In this sequence of events many fail-safe measures weren't taken. The nurse had several chances to call in the private physician and could have familiarized the resident more fully with the case, allowing him to take the baby thirty minutes sooner. The private physician could have addressed the problem in a timelier manner.

All of these—perhaps any of these—opportunities taken would have made the difference. Instead, in the end, the mother and child's lives were altered forever; a little boy has cerebral palsy, who cannot take care of himself and will not grow out of it.

The insurance company bought what peace there was with money–and the "problem" went away for those responsible. Alas, that is the best the system could offer these victims.

It is interesting that the private physician was spared having to accept a malpractice settlement which would require reporting to the National and State Data Bank. Instead, because this physician was a high producer of business for the hospital, it accepted full responsibility and paid the full settlement.

Wow, corporate manipulation at its best.

Conclusion

My journey began in the Fall of 1965 when, after being notified I'd passed the bar exam, I was thrown out of compensation court when the judge realized I wasn't yet sworn in.

The journey continues into the 21st Century. I have endeavored to use the system to aid victims in all aspects of practice; from major criminal cases through attempts at changing inadequate and/or imperfect laws, and now to perfecting personal injury and medical malpractice claims and trying to keep the NJRC within the written law.

The cases and personalities I have been involved with have provided me a broad perspective on our legal system. While the cases presented are only a small part of my practice, they are illustrative of how I spent my professional time these fifty exciting years. I see some broad generalities, and I can draw some very specific conclusions.

The system is imperfect, like any system, but especially susceptible to abuse by those with personality problems, who are lazy, or have unrealistic expectations of reality. Too often, judges do not have open minds, aren't neutral, or simply don't care. There is most certainly an "establishment" which looks to protect its status quo, demanding certain approaches and limitations on fairness and justice.

Below is a list of cases in which I participated that resulted in formal opinions. Some results were wonderful; some tragic. My comments are self-explanatory.

The list does not include some significant unreported opinions of the Appellate Division and Trial Division. The Committee on Opinions goes a long way in managing what becomes our formal to-be-cited common law.

In the end, it was worth it all to try and carry the ball for numerous clients and causes, though some didn't deserve the effort.

For me, this book is part journal and to a greater extent, an autobiography. Like my career in law, I know I must end this book. But there is a gnawing feeling that I shouldn't let go. More precisely, a feeling I don't want to.

I leave with one consistent thought: I did what a lawyer is supposed to do—get the best result he or she can for their client. Sometimes, I was pleasantly surprised with the result; sometimes bitterly disappointed.

But at the end, looking at the body of work, I have to say, "Michael, it sure was, and is, quite a trip."

Written Opinions

Supreme Court of New Jersey

Application of Walter Marvin, 53 N.J. 147 (1969); (BAD)

Horbal v. McNeil, 66 N.J. 99 (1974); (BAD)

Clayton v. Freehold Township Bd. Of Education, 67 N.J. 249 (1974); (BAD)

Long Branch Education Asso. V Board of Education, 73 N.J. 461 (1977); (FAIR)

State v. Vinegra, 73 N.J. 484 (1977); (GOOD)

Kelly v. Gwinnell, 96 N.J. 538 (1984); (GREAT)

In re Yaccarino, 101 N.J. 342 (1985); (JUDGESHIP) (POOR)

King v. New Jersey Racing Com., 103 N.J. 412 (1986); (BAD)

Gable v. Board of Trustees, 115 N.J. 212 (1989); (GOOD)

In re Yaccarino, 117 N.J. 175 (1989); (LAW LICENSE) (POOR)

In re Rogers, 126 N.J. 345 (1991); (GOOD)

In re Anis, 126 N.J. 448 (1992); (FAIR)

Herman v. Sunshine Chem. Specialties, 133 N.J. 329 (1993); (GREAT)

Ahn v. Kim, 145 N.J. 423 (1996); (GOOD)

Clohesy v. Food Circus Supermarkets, 149 N.J. 496 (1997); (GREAT)

Campione v. Soden, 150 N.J. 163 (1997); (GREAT)

Fink v. Thompson, 167 N.J. 551 (2001); (GREAT)

Gonzalez v. Ideal Tile Importing Co., 184 N.J. 415 (2005); (BAD)

DeMarco v. Stoddard, 223 N.J. 363 (2015); (THE WORST)

Superior Court of New Jersey, Appellate Division

Long Branch Div. of United Civic & Taxpayers Org. v. Cowan, 119 N.J. Super. 306 (App. Div. 1972); (GOOD)

Knapp v. Phillips Petroleum Co., 123 N.J. Super. 26 (App. Div. 1973); (GOOD)

State v. Blanton, 166 N.J. Super. 62 (App. Div. 1979); (GOOD)

State v. Curtis, 195 N.J. Super. 354 (App. Div. 1984); (BAD)

State v. Miller, 220 N.J. Super. 106 (App. Div. 1985); (GREAT)

DeVitis v. N.J. Racing Com., 202 N.J. Super. 484 (App. Div. 1985); (POOR)

New Mea Constr. Corp. v. Harper, 203 N.J. Super. 486 (App. Div. 1985); (GOOD)

Emmer v. Merin, 233 N.J. Super. 568 (App. Div. 1989); (BAD)

Moiseyev v. New Jersey Racing Com'n, 239 N.J. Super. 1 (App. Div. 1989); (GOOD)

Morella v. Machu, 235 N.J. Super. 604 (App. Div. 1989); (GREAT)

State v. Turcotte, 239 N.J. Super. 285 (App. Div. 1990); (BAD)

Russell v. Coyle, 266 N.J. Super. 651 (App. Div. 1993); (GOOD)

Insulation Corp. of America v. Berkowitz, 274 N.J. Super. 337 (App. Div. 1994); (GOOD)

McBride v. Minstar, Inc., 283 N.J. Super. 471 (Super. Ct. 1994); (BAD)

Thomas v. Toys R Us, Inc., 282 N.J. Super. 569 (App. Div. 1995); (BAD)

McBride v. Raichle Molitor, USA, 283 N.J. Super. 422 (App. Div. 1995); (BAD)

Lohmeyer v. Frontier Ins. Co., 294 N.J. Super. 547 (App. Div. 1996); (GOOD)

Underwood v. Atl. City Racing Ass'n, 295 N.J. Super. 335 (App. Div. 1996); (GOOD)

Ryan v. Lcs, Inc., 311 N.J. Super. 618 (App. Div. 1998); (BAD)

Eage/ v. Newman, 325 N.J. Super. 467 (App. Div. 1999); (BAD)

In re Consider Distribution of Casino Simulcasting Special Fund (Accumulated in 2005), 398 N.J. Super. 7 (App. Div 2008); (GOOD)

In re Veto by Governor Chris Christie of Minutes of New Jersey Racing Comm'n from June 29, 429 N.J. Super. 277 (App. Div. 2012); (BAD)

Federal Court

Hoffaman v. Jannarone, 401 F. Supp. 1095 (D.N.J. 1975)

Shiffler v. Schlesinger, 548 F.2d 96 (Jrd Cir. 1977) Shiffler v. Brown, 591 F.2d 1336 (3rd Cir. 1979) Reid v. Barrett, 467 F. Supp 124 (D.N.J. 1979) United States v. Mack, 614 F.2d 771 (3rd Cir. 1980) Reid v. Barrett, 615 F.2d 1354 (3rd Cir. 1980)

O'Biso v. Board of Education, 639 F.2d 774 (3rd Cir. 1980) Wright v. Monmouth College, 692 F.2d 750 (3rd Cir. 1982) Wright v. Monmouth College, 709 F.2d 1497 (3rd Cir. 1983) Holloway v. Whaley, 116 F.R.D. 675 (D.N.J. 1987)

Bartels v. Sports Arena Employees Local, 137, 838 F.2d 101 (3rd Cir. 1988) Walsh Sec. v. Cristo Prop Mgmt., 7 F. Supp 2d 523 (D.N.J. 1998)

Garden State Auto Park Pontiac GMC Trick, Inc. v. Electronic Data Sys Corp.,31 F. Supp 2d 378 (D.N.J. 1998)

Greenwich Life Settlements, Inc. v. Viasource Funding Group, LLC, "7-742 F. Supp 2d 446 (D.N.J. 2010)

About the Author

This son of a Monmouth County chicken farmer, since his admission to the Bar in 1965, has been an active litigator in Civil, Chancery and Criminal Courts and has appeared before various State administrative agencies. He has served as trial and appellate counsel in several pivotal and highly publicized cases, including *State v. Bruce Curtis*, a murder trial which went to the Superior Court, Appellate Division with a reported opinion that clarified the law on aggravated manslaughter which resulted in a treaty with Canada, and was the subject of a CBS television movie and several books.

Mr. Schottland has been counsel in favorable Supreme Court Decisions in *Kelly v. Gwinnell*, *Herman v. Sunshine Chemical*, *Clohesy v. Food Circus*, *Cook v. PERS*, *Fink v. Thompson*, *Ahn v. Carrier Foundation* and *Campione v. Soden*. Those matters extended liability to the host of private parties, clarified the law on punitive damages, established store owner liability for incidents in mall parking lots, clarified the law for accidental retirement pensions, malpractice matters, as well as the law of damages. These and several other reported cases established precedents in various aspects of civil tort law and administrative law matters.

Mr. Schottland has written several articles that have appeared in the New Jersey Law Journal on various topics from no-fault/verbal threshold law to comments regarding judicial evaluation and the publication of ethics matters. He has also had articles on various topics of public interest published in the New York Times and local area newspapers, the latest regarding the Kentucky Derby disqualification.

He has been a member of the Monmouth Bar Association for many years and served as Chairman of its Civil Practice Committee and is a member emeritus of the New Jersey State Bar Association.

Over his career, which has spanned more than fifty years, he has achieved several substantial and notable results in the courts. He is currently active in malpractice matters, general civil litigation and cases related to racing law. Previously he was active in public and private labor relations matters. He has served as an arbitrator in many serious matters.

He is married, the father of five children, grandfather of ten, and resides in the Borough of Shrewsbury, New Jersey with his wife, Rosanne.

Among his non-law interests and his immediate family, he has enjoyed both harness and thoroughbred racing, visits to the blackjack table, reading numerous books on politics, history, adventure and famous people. He is a life-long Red Sox fan.

Visit Michael at http://TheLegalEye.net

www.ingramcontent.com/pod-product-compliance
Lightning Source LLC
Chambersburg PA
CBHW021926040426
42448CB00008B/933